Bolivia at the Crossroads

As Bolivia reels from the collapse of the government in November 2019, a wave of social protests, and now the impact of Covid-19, this book asks: where next for Bolivia?

After almost 14 years in power, the government of Bolivia's first indigenous president collapsed in 2019 amidst widescale protest and allegations of electoral fraud. The contested transitional government that emerged was quickly struck by the impacts of the Covid-19 public health crisis. This book reflects on this critical moment in Bolivia's development from the perspectives of politics, the economy, the judiciary and the environment. It asks what key issues emerged during Evo Morales's administration and what are the main challenges awaiting the next government in order to steer the country through a new and uncertain road ahead.

As the world considers what the ultimate legacy of Morales's left-wing social experiment will be, this book will be of great interest to researchers across the fields of Latin American studies, development, politics, and economics, as well as to professionals active in the promotion of development in the country and the region.

Soledad Valdivia Rivera is Assistant Professor, Institute of History, Leiden University, the Netherlands.

Routledge Studies in Latin American Development

The series features innovative and original research on Latin American development from scholars both within and outside of Latin America. It particularly promotes comparative and interdisciplinary research targeted at a global readership.

In terms of theory and method, rather than basing itself on any one orthodoxy, the series draws broadly on the tool kit of the social sciences in general, emphasizing comparison, the analysis of the structure and processes, and the application of qualitative and quantitative methods.

Industrial Development in Mexico
Policy Transformation from Below
Walid Tijerina

The Informal Sector in Ecuador
Artisans, Entrepreneurs, and Precarious Family Firms
Alan Middleton

Development Banks and Sustainability in the Andean Amazon
Edited by Rebecca Ray, Kevin P. Gallagher and Cynthia A. Sanborn

Bolivia at the Crossroads
Politics, Economy, and Environment in a Time of Crisis
Edited by Soledad Valdivia Rivera

Legal Experiments for Development in Latin America
Modernization, Revolution and Social Justice
[illegible]ena Alviar García

[illegible] information about this series, please visit: https://www.routledge.com

Bolivia at the Crossroads

Politics, Economy, and Environment in a Time of Crisis

Edited by
Soledad Valdivia Rivera

Routledge
Taylor & Francis Group
LONDON AND NEW YORK

First published 2021
by Routledge
2 Park Square, Milton Park, Abingdon, Oxon OX14 4RN

and by Routledge
605 Third Avenue, New York, NY 10158

Routledge is an imprint of the Taylor & Francis Group, an informa business

British Library Cataloguing-in-Publication Data
A catalogue record for this book is available from the British Library

Library of Congress Cataloging-in-Publication Data
Names: Valdivia Rivera, Soledad, editor.
Title: Bolivia at the crossroads : politics, economy, and environment in a time of crisis / edited by Soledad Valdivia Rivera.
Other titles: Politics, economy, and environment in a time of crisis
Description: Abingdon, Oxon ; New York, NY : Routledge, 2021. | Series: Routledge studies in Latin American development | Includes bibliographical references and index.
Identifiers: LCCN 2020052834 (print) | LCCN 2020052835 (ebook)
Subjects: LCSH: Bolivia—Politics and government—21st century. | Bolivia—Economic policy. | Morales Ayma, Evo, 1959–
Classification: LCC F3327 .B637 2021 (print) | LCC F3327 (ebook) | DDC 984.05/4—dc23
LC record available at https://lccn.loc.gov/2020052834
LC ebook record available at https://lccn.loc.gov/2020052835

ISBN: 978-0-367-70772-9 (hbk)
ISBN: 978-0-367-70774-3 (pbk)
ISBN: 978-1-003-14792-3 (ebk)

Typeset in Times New Roman
by codeMantra

Contents

Contributors

Fabio S. M. Castro is PhD candidate in World Political Economy, Federal University of ABC, Brazil.

Sinclair M. G. Guerra is Professor of the Postgraduate Program in World Political Economy, Federal University of ABC, Brazil.

Bret Gustafson is Associate professor of Sociocultural Anthropology, Washington University, USA.

Paulo A. Lima Filho is General Coordinator of the Brazilian Institute for Contemporary Studies (IBEC), Brazil.

Angus McNelly is Honorary Research Fellow at the School of Politics and International Relations, Queen Mary University, UK.

Eduardo Rodríguez Veltzé served as president of Bolivia and as Chief Justice of the Bolivian Supreme Court, Bolivia.

Soledad Valdivia Rivera is Assistant Professor, Institute of History, Leiden University, the Netherlands.

Acknowledgements

I would like to thank all the participating authors for their invaluable contributions to the volume, and for the pleasure of collaborating with them. I would also like to thank the three anonymous readers for their insightful and constructive comments on the book's proposal that helped to improve the final result (all shortcomings are my own). A special acknowledgement goes to my colleagues at the Latin American Studies Department and the Institute of History of Leiden University, in particular to Patricio Silva. I thank Fernando, Mercedes, Zoé, Thor and Nyah, who form an interminable source of inspiration and support. I thank Håvar for truly making everything possible, unconditionally. I would also like to express my gratitude to Helena Hurd and Matt Shobbrook at Routledge for all their professional support.

Introduction

Continuity and change in the 2019–2020 Bolivian crisis

Bolivia entered a period of crisis at the end of 2019, after elections held on 20 October that year failed and the first indigenous and longest sitting president of the country, Evo Morales, was forced to resign from office amidst social protest and military pressure. Morales' ascendancy to presidency was preceded by a political crisis too. The period 2000–2005 saw a sequence of episodes of social insurgence in which popular social movements, particularly around pro-indigenous and anti-liberal demands, ousted president Gonzalo Sánchez de Lozada in 2003 and Carlos Mesa in 2005, deriving in a transitional government led by Eduardo Rodríguez Veltzé. Morales' party, the Movement towards Socialism (MAS), booked a landslide victory in the December 2005 elections, promising radical political, social, economic and cultural transformations.

The almost 14 years of the MAS government under the leadership of Evo Morales, having won the 2009 and 2014 elections with over 60% of the vote, have sparked hot debates around its achievements, limitations and misapprehensions. There is relative consensus about the significant transformations the have resulted of the very ambitious progressive agenda, including the drafting and promulgation of a new constitution in 2009, the nationalization of key sectors of the economy, the revindication of the indigenous and the reduction of poverty. The MAS government has received recognition particularly for its sound economic policy. However, there has also been much critique, pointing towards an undermining and deterioration of democratic institutions and increasing authoritarianism, corruption, poor environmental policy and an uneven and contradictory inclusion of indigenous constituencies. Both praise and condemnation have been particularly directed to the address of Evo Morales. In line with the presidentialism that characterizes the Latin American region, Morales' mark seems deep indeed. Upon his return to Bolivia, after a year of exile, he continues to be referred to as *hermano presidente* (brother president) and the persistent weight of his leadership is attested by the emotive welcome given by the multitude that gathered for his homecoming in the Chapare region on 9 November 2020. However, Morales evoked equally intense feelings of rejection a year before when thousands of people marched the streets of the urban centres of Bolivia, demanding his resignation. After his demise, the right-wing transitional government of Jeanine Áñez continuously celebrated the recuperation of democracy and the end of the prolonged 'dictatorship' of Morales, a discourse that resonated with large segments of the population. In that way, even upon the return of the MAS to power with 55% of the vote in the 2020 elections, the removal of Morales from the presidential seat arguably constitutes a turning point.

But the crossroads at which Bolivia stands involves much more than the change of a president. The political scenario is but one of the dimensions of the crisis. The increased political polarization has served to reignite and exacerbate long-standing ethnic, regional and cultural fissures that add a significant social layer to the Bolivian schism. In addition, weak environmental policy and the expansion of the agro-industry sector supported by the MAS government have incentivized the recurring practice of the burning of forest land in the Amazon basin, resulting in the largest fires in Bolivia's recent history in 2019 and 2020, an environmental disaster. The Covid-19 pandemic has caused around 9,000 deaths according to official numbers, but studies suggest the real number could be as much as six times higher, situating Bolivia amongst the worst-hit countries in the Latin American region and in the world (DW 2020, France24 2020). Besides the severe health situation, the Covid-19 has had a major impact on the domestic economy, particularly affecting the popular sectors in the informal economy as well as the small- and middle-scale enterprises, while the sustained effects on the global economy have had a negative effect on the heavy-weight export-oriented sectors.

Bolivia stands before a truly multifaceted crisis. The transparency and order that characterized the 2020 election should be acknowledged as a democratic triumph, but the long road that led to that moment was marked by hostility, tension, violence, misrule and uncertainty, and so its final outcome was by no means self-evident. It demonstrates that the overwhelming majority of the Bolivians opted, in tense calmness, for a democratic way out of the political crisis. It also shows that a 55% majority sees in the MAS the best bet to face the multiple challenges ahead, which constitutes a clear message that gives the Arce government a high level of legitimacy and trust to steer the country forward. These are both important and positive developments but, at the end of the day, they may not amount to much more than the minimal conditions to address the structural problems and the complicated political decisions ahead.

The fall of Evo Morales: coup d'état or citizen revolt?

The longest presidency of Bolivia came to an abrupt end on 12 November 2019 when Evo Morales resigned office amidst military pressure. The national elections held on 19 October 2019 had given Morales 47% of the vote, ten points above the challenging candidate Carlos Mesa, barely enough to avoid a second round, thus securing his fourth presidential term. But allegations of electoral fraud quickly spread on the election night. A mysterious interruption occurred in the unofficial rapid computing system stopping the actualization of the voter turnout as local results kept coming in. The system was restored 24 hours later showing a much larger gap between Morales and Mesa than it had depicted before the sudden interruption, just enough to prevent a run off. In the following days citizens mobilized in the Bolivian urban centres, denouncing the electoral fraud and demanding Morales resignation. This growing protest was soon met with mobilizations of supporters of Morales, defending his electoral victory. Morales requested an audit by the Organization of American States (OAS) and promised to call for new elections if fraud was detected.

The preliminary report of the OAS arrived on 12 November having found too many irregularities to endorse the election results. From that point the situation quickly deteriorated. Morales' call for fresh elections was not able to appease the social insurgence. A mutiny under the police force that had started the day before severely weakened Morales' position. Upon the result of the OAS audit, the military 'suggested' Morales to resign and reports turned up of higher-up MAS officials being pressured to leave office by burning their houses and threatening their family members. An interim government was quickly installed, as ice-president of the senate, Jeanine Áñez, assumed office in a questionable constitutional succession, following the resignation of various MAS representatives. Supporters of MAS and Morales organized protests against the coup d'état that were answered with harsh military force resulting in over 20 casualties amongst Morales supporters. Particularly the incidents in Senkata and Sacaba showed disproportionate use of violence, leading various instances to denounce severe violations of human rights (see particularly International Human Rights Clinic 2020).

Jonas Wolff (2020) offers a comprehensive review of the academic literature regarding the question of electoral fraud and the coup controversy, including all major technical reports. On the first point it concludes that, although serious irregularities occurred, the evidence put forward for intentional manipulation is limited and contested, and certainly does not prove massive fraud. However, given the thin margin by which Morales would avoid a second round, it is plausible that fraud made a decisive difference (pp. 174–175). On the second point, it concludes that in terms of procedure constitutional order was maintained while, substantially speaking, various elements attest to the undemocratic nature of the transition, not least of which was the open and drastic contradiction to the popular will (p. 177). Balanced and careful, these inferences remain inconclusive, reflecting that the answer to these questions is not to be found in factual or technical accounts but on the interpretation of facts and technicalities. Those that conclude fraud occurred, emphasize the irregularities and the plausibility of its effect on the final result, while those that contest it emphasize that there is no evidence of intentional and massive manipulation, and that results correspond with statistical analysis. On the second point, the conclusion that a constitutional and democratic transition took place in November 2019 ascribes determinant value to a strict legal procedure endorsed by the Constitutional Court, while those that support the coup assign conclusive power to the (violent) pressure exerted on the authorities, particularly by the police and the military, that forced the premature end of their constitutional terms.

In short, the polemic reflects the complexity and confusing nature of the October-November 2019 events and demonstrates that there is room for discussion and interpretation. And this is exactly what Bolivians have done from the very beginning. In October 2019, while the government was looking for an institutional way out of the evolving political crisis, awaiting the results of the audit by the OAS, the streets were considerably less conciliatory. On 28 October, thousands of people gathered in the wealthier southern district of the city of La Paz to denounce the electoral fraud and demand Morales' resignation. At the exact same time, in the adjacent El Alto, a city that grew out of indigenous rural immigrants in search of jobs in the capital, an equally large concentration of people gathered in support of Morales. They denounced that the election and Morales' victory was being stolen. This was not a coincidence. Both sides turned to the streets as a way to measure the strength and legitimacy of their position by the number of people each interpretation was able to mobilize on the streets. The concentrations of 28 October are, in a way, characteristic of how many of the most important political discussions have been held in the recent history of Bolivia. For example, the 2017 ruling by the Constitutional Court that allowed for Morales' fourth presidential candidature was surrounded by mobilizations both in its favour and rejection. Although, formally speaking, his fourth candidature was 'legal' by the endorsement of the Constitutional Court, large segments of the population saw it as a tricky scheme by which Morales sought to 'perpetuate' himself in power and, although ultimately celebrated, it could not prevent from being intuitively frowned upon by Morales sympathizers and supporters. The 28 October protest in La Paz illustrates how the deep polarization that had marked the run up to the election ultimately crystalized into two competing narratives: 'fraud vs. coup'. In this scenario, the questions, far from being a matter of investigation, were from the beginning a matter of opinion and political positioning.

Arguably, the schism in Bolivian society is an element of continuity throughout Bolivian history, which varies in the form and intensity of its expression in time. The various historical and structural divisions inherent in Bolivian society, in a way, collapsed into the two competing narratives of electoral fraud-civil revolt vs. the coup d'état, with powerful and significant mobilizing effects in the struggle to obtain political power. Bolivia was submerged in an electoral campaign that started mid-2019 and only ended in October 2020. As is usual with electoral periods, for over a year the public debate sought to maximize differences and contrast the political options, which were arguably two, MAS and anti-MAS, rendering the division more explicit and more profound. As a matter of political opinion, in 2020 Bolivians voted as much on the 'fraud vs. coupe' issue as on the candidates, if not more so. The candidature of interim president Jeanine Áñez should be interpreted in this way. As she assumed power, she promised not to pursue electoral ambitions but by January 2020 her rising popularity rates pushed the launch of her candidature. A portion of the population saw in Áñez the promise of continuity of the democratizing process that had started with the ousting of Morales, while others saw a confirmation of the ambitions of power that had forcefully removed Morales. Even Carlos Mesa, who had openly supported the transition, stated that Áñez candidature validated the coup d'état thesis (Mesa 2020). By September, it was clear that an ever-smaller portion of the population believed in a democratic role of Áñez in Bolivia's past and future, leading her to withdraw from the electoral race to prevent further dispersion of the anti-MAS vote amidst an imminent victory of that political option (ANF 2020). In the same vein, the results of the 2020 election can be read as the expression of the division between those who believe they have recovered democracy after a year of the de facto government by Jeanine Áñez, and those who believe they enacted a successful civil upsurge against the authoritarian regime of Evo Morales and for whom the return of the MAS to power constitutes a democratic regression. Although the 2020 elections are deemed a democratic success, they have not fundamentally altered this social fracture.

While the 2020 elections signal a partial emergence of the political crisis, the new government faces large challenges including the management of the pandemic and the reactivation of the economy. The necessary measures will only be viable if they can build on public trust and support. The much-needed consensus requires a certain level of reconciliation to create the space in which political differences can be set aside in favour of dialogue and negotiation, and in pursuit of the common interest. In that way, the 2019–2020 crisis constitutes a transition to a new and trying scenario, the crossroads at which Bolivia stands.

Aims and structure

The present volume takes the 2019–2020 crisis as the starting point, to address in a timely and concise manner the poignant questions of why the transition happened and what will be the forces and factors affecting the future. Through the prism of the crisis, the volume identifies and analyses underlying origins of fragmentation and transition that help make sense of the baffling events of October–November 2019 and will continue to be central in the coming conjuncture. It does so by identifying five key themes that meet three criteria: (a) it was central during the 14 years of the Morales administration, (b) it played a significant role in the 2019–2020 crisis and the transitional government, and (c) it is expected to be significant in the trying scenario post the 2020 elections.

Arguably, no work of this kind can be comprehensive, especially if it aims to be timely and concise. In addition, given the complexities of the Latin American scenarios, to which the pandemic has added extra uncertainty and to which Bolivia is no exception, venturing to future scenarios is close to fortune telling. In that sense, the book does not pretend to offer a clear and complete answer as to which direction Bolivia will turn at this crossroads. But by discussing the key issues and their role in the 2019–2020 crisis, identifying the continuity and change of factors and forces, the crisis analysis unveils the achievements and limitation of the MAS government while creating an insight into the challenges ahead. As such, the volume offers a strong base from which to read Bolivia's development in the near future. In this manner, the crisis presents itself as a 'constitutive moment' in the sense by Bolivian thinker René Zavaleta (1986), a moment of political and social de-articulation that allows tracing the elements that will shape the new social conjuncture.

Chapter 1 opens the analysis with the contribution by former Bolivian president, Eduardo Rodríguez Veltzé, where he discusses the role of the 2009 constitution in the historical pendular movement by which Bolivia swings back and forth between democracy and ochlocracy (mob rule). The chapter provides a detailed analysis of how the 2009 constitution, despite all the praise it has received, has shaped political institutions in a way that turns them incapable of canalizing and solving public dissent, falling prey to *caudillismo* politics. As such, the 2009 constitution constitutes an underlying cause for recurrent conflict including the 2019–2020 crisis. The analysis develops the argument of constitutional failure in which 'constitutional' is taken in its wider meaning, referring not only to the codified laws that define the structure of the state but encompassing the ways in which the state and society interact. The analysis finds substance in the scholarly reflection as much as in the author's personal experiences at Bolivia's highest offices (including the Supreme Court and the Presidency itself), examining the factors which led to the failure of constitutional order in 2019 and exploring the possibilities to overcome the democratic-ochlocratic pendulum.

Chapter 2 identifies social movements as the legitimate vehicles of citizen representation and participation in Bolivian politics. The chapter unveils the critical nature of the state-social movements' relation to understanding the underlying developments that lead up to the 2019–2020 crisis and making sense of the events of October-November 2019. It first traces the relation between the MAS government and its base of support in the popular (indigenous) social movements from 2010, characterizing it as effective in containing oppositional forces but gradually deteriorating. More importantly, it discusses the rise of a plurality of 'opposition' social movements around different demands amongst the (upper) middle-class and elite associated with the right wing, differentiating between those that answer to democratic grievances and those that reflect vested interests. The chapter shows the influential role of social protest, rendering any political force unable to govern without 'contentious power'. It concludes that the Bolivian political experiment continues to look for effective ways to incorporate social movements in the political process, to canalize citizen demands and avoid polarization.

The third chapter, by Angus McNelly, adopts René Zavaleta's epistemology of crisis to investigate the medium-term processes of subsumption, class formation and nation-building from a political economy perspective, identifying the origin and lineage of the socio-historical blocs behind the two competing narratives of fraud vs. coup d'état. It first discusses the contradictions created by the development model pursued by MAS that undermined support for the government amongst the urban middle classes, the upward mobile working-class and the indigenous communities affected by extractivism and infrastructure projects. It then turns to a discussion on the achievements and limitations of the Plurinational model as a nation-building project in relation to the emergence of a regional autonomy movement as its political negation. Together, the process of class formation and nation-building marked the amalgamation of socio-historical blocs into the two competing narratives that framed the struggle of the crisis.

Bret Gustafson's analysis is centred around the contemporary political struggles over land, characterizing the Áñez government as a direct representative of wealthy landowners. The chapter first assesses the land policy under the Morales government, tracing the development from a more progressive stance between 2006 and 2012 to one being marked by concessions to the eastern agro-industrial elite in the period between 2013 and 2019. The analysis examines the issue in four areas: gender and land, the battle over GMOs, the fires in the Amazon and Indigenous territorial autonomies while attesting to transversal environmental effects. It then discusses the various ways in which the interim government advanced the interest of the agro-industrial elite of the east. The chapter shows how the resistance to extractivism has not been able to formulate alternative political visions of agricultural production and, more important, that attempts to change the current structure of land use pass by the unlikely dismantling of a hegemonic bloc connected to global agro-capital. In this way, the 2019–2020 crisis also reflects a clash between the interests of nature and human well-being and those of multinational capital.

The forceful removal of Morales from power ignited speculation on the role of the large lithium reserves. As early as 2008, the Morales government had started to delineate a clear strategy for the extraction and industrialization of this mineral, as the country is known to possess the largest reserves. As the main raw material for the production of batteries, the world demand for lithium is expected to rise exponentially amidst the global energy transition, first due to the harsh competition in the electric vehicles market, and then because of the need of powerful batteries to enable the revolutionary 5G technology. In this way, Bolivia's lithium appears to be standing in the midst of the hegemonic dispute between the United States and China. The chapter traces Bolivia's contradictory attempt at overcoming underdevelopment and reasserting sovereignty, through the indigenous worldview of 'living well' while building on historical structures of extractivism. The chapter discusses the main tenets of the lithium strategy, its progress and the impediments it encounters to conclude that the Arce government stands before the challenge to recover 'living well' as the horizon of the way forward.

More than the sum of its parts

Although each of the contributions stands on its own and can be read separately in whatever order, the volume as presented here amounts to more than the sum of its parts. By connecting around their role in explaining the crisis, the central themes of the chapters reveal the intertwined developments, forces and actors. In this way, the five themes – the 2009 constitution, social movements, class, land and lithium – each tracing long-term developments, offer multiple perspectives and unveil the surfacing transversal factors and forces.

The state-society relation is an underlying factor in Chapters 1–3. By its analysis of the 2009 Constitution, Chapter 1 observes that the state institutions continue to be instruments of collective dominance rather than acting as consent-seeking actors. An important difference is that the collective dominance is no longer exerted by the white economic elites, but lays in the hands of (indigenous) popular collectives. This dysfunction renders institutional politics unable to find a solution to the conflict, leading to recurrent outbursts of ochlocracy. The salient role of social movements is an expression of this, where the deficient representation of social groups at the level of institutions, has pushed demands outside of it, to the realm of street politics. The historically marginalized indigenous and popular sectors protested against the exclusionary state under neoliberalism, producing the cycles of mobilization that brought Evo Morales to power. Although the 2009 constitution certainly establishes the institutional inclusion and greater representation of the historically marginalized, it appears to have been unable to change the historical nature of the state as an instrument of collective domination. The social movement serves as an effective and legitimate vehicle of citizen participation and representation that compensates this deficiency. Under the 14 years of the administration of Morales, old and new grievances have been articulated through this means. Chapter 3 traces the lineage of grievances in the long-term formation of socio-historical blocs and state nation-building projects as processes of class formation and alliances.

The rise of right-wing forces expressed in the 2019–2020 crisis is another transversal dimension of the joint analysis. Chapter 1 sees in the 2009 constitution the displacement of the historical dominance of the white economic elite. Having lost its privileged position in the realm of institutional politics, this force has shifted to street politics (Chapter 2), particularly as a regional autonomy movement linked to the agro-industry's vested interests (Chapter 3), forming the backbone of the opposition to MAS. Chapter 4 deepens the analysis of this force by looking at its role in the crisis from the long perspective of the historical issue of land in Bolivia, identifying the use of Genetically Modified Organisms (GMO) as the base of fascism and characterizing the Áñez government as the capturing of the state by the agrarian elite of the eastern region of Bolivia.

The chapters also identify the indigenous as the central force in Bolivia's development. The 2009 constitution reflects the struggle for indigenous emancipation, aiming at reversing the historical exclusion from the national projects (Chapter 1). Indigenous values act as guiding principles in concrete and strategic policy, where the lithium strategy is meant to create the material conditions to transcend capital and move towards 'living well' (Chapter 5). Indigenous movements were key in bringing the MAS government to power; they form the important base of support that kept it in power for almost 14 years and that brought it back in 2020. They represent the most consolidated of the plurality of social movements in contemporary Bolivia (Chapter 2). However, as the analysis shows, the 'indigenous' is not a solid block but a category that encompasses much heterogeneity, explaining its nature as a continuous source of resistance in defence of their rights and territory, particularly in relation to large infrastructural projects (Chapters 2–5).

In relation to the above the issue of the environment, as one dimension of the crisis, appears intertwined in the five central themes compounding this book. In Bolivia, the issue of the environment holds a strong connection with the indigenous worldviews, as it has been framed as the protection of the rights of Mother Earth. In that way, the subjugation of nature to development appears as the most important contradiction of the MAS administration, particularly by its extractivist policies. The case of the lithium strategy is emblematic in this sense. The extraction of lithium (Chapter 5) is meant to create the material conditions to transition to 'living well', but it constitutes an activity that will cause high environmental damage, and that will threaten local indigenous population's access to water (water is needed in large quantities for the extraction). Thus, the pursuit of 'living well' enters in direct contradiction with the rights of indigenous peoples and of Mother Earth. The environmental effects of the current agrarian use of land in eastern Bolivia are also identified as problematic, in the use of GMOs and also in the expansion of the agricultural frontier. Over the years, the MAS government has diluted its once progressive land policy, creating the conditions for the devastating forest fires in 2019 and 2020 (Chapter 4). As such, environmental concerns have been powerful in articulating social protest (Chapters 2, 3 and 5), but less in formulating political alternatives for land policy (Chapter 4) and for extractivist strategies (Chapter 5).

Last, the combined analysis points to the international dimension of the domestic crisis. Dependency structures have conditioned and continue to condition Bolivian paths to development, impacting the formation of socio-historical blocs (Chapter 3). The contribution of Bret Gustafson reveals the connections between extractivism and global capital and markets through the powerful agro-industrial elite that captured the state after the removal of Morales. The MAS government's previous conciliatory concessions in land and environmental policy can also be seen as responding to the need to balance the pressure exerted by global capital. Chapter 5 takes a more explicit geopolitical analysis to the role of lithium, in which Bolivia's attempt to reassert sovereignty in entering the global markets amidst a global energy transition, has situated the country at the core of global hegemonic disputes, affecting domestic affairs and attempts to overcome dependency and underdevelopment.

The contributions have been constrained in the extension, following the aim of producing a concise and timely assessment of the crisis. In this way, although certainly not comprehensive, the volume offers a wide-range and in-depth, yet succinct understanding of the 2019–2020 crisis, that builds on an assessment of the achievements and limitations of the almost 14 years of MAS government under the leadership of Evo Morales, and that hints at the challenges ahead. The multiple perspectives do justice to the complexity and controversy surrounding the crisis, revealing the intersections among the underlying themes while attesting to their significance for Bolivia's past and future.

References

ANF (2020) 'Tras bajo apoyo en encuestas, Jeanine Añez declina candidatura a la Presidencia', 17 September. https://www.noticiasfides.com/nacional/politica/tras-bajo-apoyo-en-encuestas-jeanine-anez-declina-candidatura-a-la-presidencia--406353?__cf_chl_jschl_tk__=f64c50e2e006eff7d1fcba02b30995cb19677ad2-1605454412-0-AYJq3kAMg2YaYGshcVFfvYMsnXy0SIgX5b4J7gfIyUlXN8gOMzL9QzQEwqjySkKLUyWNw9ESdN7GTPDQFyeoiVofwMEsYA6g4p38xr1DaWuCzyBe7f6xycVUuqvIo05MjZiNdmwmJzRMsbC3VC_SqEQ-PlRyzU4-g5Ug2BMy_GRyCuFr8UUjGDZWatE88gZE8bgRY5ad7vENW8ah5xyDK1WbDW3VWNzmQCxDl1VYLVUgwg_JcWsWmF0_yPkeOAAa_InekAF4OfMJv9a-t-K42C_ITbJVPs30_-OOk1ulJr7K4dh6PGXEpPXiL1zwaq6mvGPWpn-KDKOBQP-sArJH18ljeDiVovf7FaNkd9UJ0Flqtb65X_WlZPAaE-J0ema5ZyGkwBdjrz8ByVyymQYSutZ9qO4wVxFhVyBHylhgdWKn

DW (2020) 'Bolivia bate récord diario de muertes por coronavirus', 9 September. https://www.dw.com/es/bolivia-bate-r%C3%A9cord-diario-de-muertes-por-coronavirus/a-54799639

France24 (2020) 'La vuelta al mundo: alarmantes cifras de letalidad por Covid-19 en Brasil, Perú y Bolivia', 6 November. https://www.france24.com/es/am%C3%A9rica-latina/20201106-vuelta-mundo-letalidad-brasil-peru-bolivia

International Human Rights Clinic (2020) *"The Shot Us Like Animals". Black November & Bolivia's Interim Government.* http://hrp.law.harvard.edu/wp-content/uploads/2020/07/Black-November-English-Final_Accessible.pdf

Mesa, C.D. (2020) 'Una decisión equivocada', *Página Siete*, 26 January. https://www.paginasiete.bo/opinion/carlos-d-me-sa/2020/1/26/una-decision-equivocada-244591.html

Wolf, J. (2020). 'The Turbulent End of an Era in Bolivia: Contested Elections, the Ouster of Evo Morales, and the Beginning of a Transition towards an Uncertain Future', *Revista de Ciencia Política*, vol 40, no 2, pp 163–186.

Zavaleta, R. (1986) *Lo nacional-popular en Bolivia.* Siglo XXI, Mexico.

1 From democracy to an ochlocratic intermission

The 2009 Constitution in the Bolivian pendulum

Eduardo Rodríguez Veltzé

Introduction

Constitutional failure best describes the situation in Bolivia at the end of 2019. The academic discourse around the subject is split between those who seek to prove that a coup against president Evo Morales took place and those who see a civic, pro-democracy movement displacing his increasingly authoritarian and illegitimate rule. Following Morales' ousting by the armed forces and the police as a result of the failed elections of October 2019 amid fraud allegations and social unrest, the questioned interim presidency of Jeanine Áñez soon mismanaged its time in office. Her government exerted unnecessary violence by the armed forces and the police to halt public demonstrations and failed to respond effectively to the COVID-19 pandemic. Áñez attempted to profiteer from an untimely presidential candidacy and she delayed the rerun of elections twice.

New elections were satisfactorily held in October 2020. A clear majority of Bolivians have chosen to hand the government to Luis Arce as president, and David Choquehuanca as vice-president. Both were Evo Morales' former economic and foreign affairs ministers, respectively. The MAS-IPSP party won with a comfortable majority[1] as if to dispel any doubt of the population's yearning for stability and clarity in politics.

It has been debated whether the end of Mr Morales represented a democratic spring against an ever more authoritarian and illegitimate regime, or whether it was a coup d'état by the reactionary right. Neither of these premises fully captures the upheaval that Bolivia went through at the end of 2019. A breakdown of constitutional order made me president in 2005 (The New York Times 2005). A chain of successive resignations started in 2003 when president Gonzalo Sánchez de Lozada left Bolivia after the social upheaval left dozens of dead victims as a result of civilian and armed forces confrontations. Carlos Mesa, his vice-president and successor was not able to address their grievances nor was he able to coordinate with the Legislative Congress, a structural governance agenda, on key issues like passing a new hydrocarbons law or calling a constitutional convention. People were out in the streets claiming a renewal of a decayed political system embedded in the Executive and the Legislative offices whose leaders were also moved to decline the presidential succession. Given some similarities between then and now, I will outline the flaws of Bolivian rule of law and its political system that led to its constitutional failure in 2019.

Historically Bolivia is one of the countries that have had the most revolutions and coups worldwide (Coup d'etat Dataset). Throughout time, since the Independence in 1825, social convulsion has ousted governments and military dictatorships have interrupted democratic practices. While the country holds mostly free and fair elections, political parties exist and democratic practices are widespread, street protests often derail the formal proceeding of the formal democratic procedure. This makes Bolivia a Janus-faced democracy, to put it in classical terms. In antiquity, Plato outlined dichotomies of different types of government. Differentiating by the number of people who ruled, Plato defined democracy as the virtuous rule 'kratos' of the people in general, the 'demos'. But the rule of the people also had a problematic side. Plato referred to the 'bad' side of democracy as the rule of the mob: ochlocracy. Both forms of democratic rule can be found throughout Bolivian history.

Bolivia has a tradition of democratic values and principles worth the name, but popular dissent has not been properly channeled through the State's institutions. This has resulted in episodes where the masses (or mobs) have taken over public space forcing governments into action, attempting to take over tacit power, basically ruling over the country themselves. Despite these abrupt changes in political procedure, Bolivia has shown the ability to swing from one type of democratic practice to the other, with the utmost flexibility. The last 38 years of democracy have been the longest period of continued democratic rule, despite its ups and downs, if we consider the ochlocratic intermissions also as a form of democratic rule. This is a persistent state of upheaval, nonetheless. It is the source of the lack of good governance, specifically caused by a broken system of checks and balances, a missing independent and effective judicial system and a predatory presidentialism resulting in a democratic-ochlocratic pendulum.

Following this line of thought, Bolivia's current woes deepen in their scope. The delayed elections after the 2019 crisis to replace the executive and legislative branches may be seen to correct the current extraordinary lack of political legitimacy in the country. Following the lack of positive legitimacy of the Áñez presidency, the elections held are but a short-term solution to the issues at hand. Mere elections do not address the fact that the constitution and the four main organs of the State failed catastrophically in 2019.

With this introduction I want to develop the argument of constitutional failure. At first glance this may sound narrowly legal, yet seen through the prism of Bolivian history, the wider meaning of the term 'constitutional' is also to be considered. As opposed to 'constitutional' meaning the codified laws that define the structures of a State, 'constitutional', when employed not only in the sense of the composition of a State but as the way the State interacts with the society that makes it up, a layer of meaning that transcends legality can be conveyed by the term. Hence 'constitutional' can be used to 'describe the [...] Constitution in terms, not of first principles but of the real behavior of those who operate it' (Crossman 1966). Accordingly, it is necessary to examine the factors that led to the failure of the constitutional order both in legal and governance-related terms in order to explore a way forward to solve the structural issue of Bolivia's democratic-ochlocratic pendulum.

Historical development and the challenges facing constitutional order in Bolivia

Bolivia was founded in 1825. The first Constitution was drafted in Lima, Peru, in 1826 and included notes from Simon Bolivar, after whom the country was named. It merely lasted five years. Since 1831, the Bolivian State has seen constitutional change by different means (either through assemblies, amendments or legislative congresses) on 15 different occasions, the last one being the Constitutional Assembly of 2006, which yielded today's constitutional text, ratified in 2009 (Rodríguez Veltzé 2008). The new Bolivian Constitution brought major conceptual and institutional innovations, framed under what is known as the 21st Century Constitutionalism in the region. This current notably focuses on granting indigenous peoples and the rural constituencies more social and political participation within the State that is traditionally run by dominant white minorities since the end of Spanish colonial rule.

Constitutionalism has become an integral part of the Bolivian State. Rojas Tudela argues that in Bolivia, since the last constitutional convention, the constitutional process can be understood as a rolling 'constitutional policy' maker, aiming at reinventing or interpreting the law in a process where the Constitution is not a unitary text but a sort of 'navigation map' with multiple options (Rojas Tudela 2018). Yet this vast history of experimentation and implementation of constitutional codification has not provided the political and societal results to establish sustainable democratic institutions that harnessed public grievances within its formally outlined systems (Gargarella 2011). Constitutionalism is a current academic and political challenge in Bolivia, because of the two main challenges faced by the 2009 constitution that stemmed from it: flawed institutions and *caudillismo*.

Arguably, Bolivia has become more inclusive since the 2009 Constitution. The ethnic and cultural diversity of the Bolivians is nowadays recognized and cherished by the State. The constitution of 2009 has provisions that revindicate those that had been systematically kept at the margin of national development throughout the country's history. Bolivia now recognizes a plethora of formerly marginalized groups (racial minorities, indigenous communities and the like) that have been given wide-ranging self-determination rights and that are now included in all matters of State. Yet, while progress has been made, Bolivia remains a postcolonial State bound by its origins as a foreign imposition of statehood on natives in their own territories. Indeed, the Bolivian State's history is one of conflict and cooperation between the newly arrived and ancestral people with whom the State institution has always operated with tacit and uninterrupted dominance of the white settlers throughout the last four centuries. This has formed the basis for the exclusion of swathes of the population from statehood. This historical legacy was interrupted by the MAS' rule from 2006. The electoral victory of indigenous political movements needs to be understood in relation to the ever-growing expansion of political rights and inclusiveness advanced since the return of democracy at the beginning of the 80s. Nevertheless, the growth in numbers and diversity of those involved in politics has not yet necessarily translated into more democratic participants. Frustration with democracy is still widespread due to persistent poverty and lack of opportunities, now starkly increased by the economic fallout due to the pandemic.

The frustration with democratic institutions, in tandem with economic difficulty, has produced the second powerful force that haunts the State-society relation: *caudillismo*. It has taken hold over political debate, where single figures, and not general ideas carried by political groups, in theory empowered by the Constitution, are the basis for political debate. Identity politics and devotion to a specific charismatic leader are the current modus operandi of political struggle.

Political leaders sell the idea that they are the organic expression of the popular will or a collective. Hereby they alone can interpret it and are legitimized solely by the acclaim they receive. In this way, serious deliberation of any kind falls second to popularity contests. Furthermore, *caudillismo* is built into the State's structure in the form of the overmighty presidency.

Since political debate is settled by popularity, the presidency is the ultimate prize and authority. Constitutional tradition has always reflected this reality. The figure of the president as the head of government and State makes the officeholder an indispensable part of the workings of the State, but also overburdens him or her with a wide range of duties. On average, the office of the president is entrusted with 30 different chores[2] which, in my personal experience, surpass a single individual's capabilities. Beyond this, the presidency does not have an underlying effective administrative structure to facilitate the process of governing. Most duties are relegated to the Ministry of the Presidency, which works with the other ministries and State organs. In addition, the president must also fulfill State representation duties and implement political goals.

The heavy-duty presidential role lacks, however, a crucial aspect, namely a relationship of cooperation with the legislative branch. The relationship between the presidency and the Legislative Assembly is currently reduced to a yearly presentation of an annual report which is not debated and has no real consequence. This leaves the presidency lacking any sort of oversight, at least within the constitutional structure. This, in combination with the need to gain and maintain popularity emanating from a political culture of *caudillismo*, accounts for the development of powerful tools to boost the image of the president when needed.

The allocation of land is exemplary for these purely popularity-enhancing tools at the disposition of the presidency. Since colonial times, the Spanish King granted entitlements in which his signature constituted the legitimation for rulers in the Americas. The postcolonial Republic retained this practice throughout the reforms and redrafts of the Constitution. Attribution 172.27 of the 2009 Constitution grants the president authority over the Bolivian Service for Agrarian Reform, which basically gives this office sole authority to grant and distribute rural property titles. Anecdotally, I remember that during my tenure in 2005 I found thousands of pending property titles, merely missing a presidential signature. This was due to the practice of withholding the titles until an opportunity to use them politically would present itself, especially with regard to large areas in the countryside. The purpose was to hold big rallies where the titles would be handed out by the president, generating great publicity. Worse still, it was rumored that previous presidents singlehandedly signed the titles. Aghast at this archaic practice, I arranged for mechanical signature devices to be used to tackle that shameful backlog. Fifteen years on, the practice is still in use. The Constitutional Assembly did not change this when working on the draft that was approved in 2009, thus retaining one of the many perennial ills of *caudillo*-style presidentialism.

The Constitution of 2009

It can be argued that any type of rule emanating from the 2009 constitution is fundamentally problematic. Yet, to assess why the constitutional structures fail to produce a stable political system that settles societal disagreement peacefully, the following question must be asked: who does what for whom? The tradition of constitutionalism, as previously outlined, has produced considerations over a number of substantive matters. A fundamental one is the problematic splintering of society in identity-based groupings. Despite the rhetorical wording of the new Constitution Preamble and articles on integration and unity of peoples, the recognition of identity-based groupings and the principles of unity do not become fully engaged in soothing deliberative processes. This, in turn, leads to a reduced or hindered authentic democratic participation, especially in the context of an immature political system and dysfunctional political parties. This results in the cooptation of these identity-based groups by charismatic leaders which vie against each other in what appears as strict popularity contests in order to reach the over-mighty presidency: an institution overburdened by tasks yet unrestricted in its power. Whereas the innovative character that some of these arrangements carry is laudable, their implementation is significantly limited by the structural issues at hand. The rest of this section discusses the roles of constitutional actors, their aims and duties.

Citizens as addressees

Starting with the last part of the question – 'For whom?' – it is necessary to specify who is the addressee of the constitutional order. Primarily, that is the subject of a constitution, and thus the addressees are the Bolivian citizenry. In this regard, Article 3 of the Constitution determines that 'the Bolivian nation is composed by the totality of Bolivians, the nations and indigenous [...] peoples [...]'. Furthermore,

Article 141 determines that Bolivian nationality is acquired by birth or naturalization. The problem is that the differentiation of legal citizens and indigenous peoples brings into question whether the applicability of the constitution is different for those who are *not* members of indigenous groups or so on, but are *merely* Bolivians.

This issue arises from Artitcle 1 St.1 whereby the Bolivian State is constituted as a 'Unitary Social State of Plurinational Communitarian Law' (Estado Unitario Social de Derecho Plurinacional Comunitario) that is free, independent, sovereign, democratic, intercultural, decentralized and with autonomies. Bolivia is founded on plurality and on political, economic, juridical, cultural and linguistic pluralism in the integration process of the country. Traditionally democracy is understood to be the rule of the people by the people, but this principle turns complex when 'the people' consists of a plurality of peoples with different rights in the same polity. The Plurinational State counts with not only citizens but also 'precolonial nations and indigenous peoples', as stated in Article 2. Furthermore, the 2009 Constitution also encompasses these groups' autonomous self-determination and autonomous regions, as well as principles of pluralism and interculturalism that operate in parallel to governing through law. This turns the constitution to merely ***a*** (but not ***the***) will of the people, as the government is then not only bound to the legislation emanating from the political processes within the framework of the constitution but coexists with parallel expressions of the will of the people. This complicated premise for the determination of who makes up the State is still being debated in the application of a plural and diverse set of rights. Furthermore, even though Article 410 provides that the Constitution is the supreme law of Bolivia and enjoys supremacy before any other normative, Article 190 allows nations and native indigenous rural peoples to exercise jurisdiction and apply their own principles, cultural values, norms and procedures. If there is a plurality of addressees who can pursue distinct goals within the State with distinct structures and procedures, unity is questionable at best and requires a fair understanding and practice of legal pluralism.

Jorge Lazarte (2015) argues that indigenous collective rights have historic legitimacy and should be protected and defended; yet such recognition does not suppose a merger between the State and collectives. The State does not become what it distinguishes nor can it be used politically to create an indigenous power project, as had happened in the past with workers and the proletariat ruling proposals. In this regard, in Article 3 the Bolivian Nation is constituted by indigenous nations and groups (again among others) together with the non-qualifying totality of all remaining Bolivian 'people'. This concept of plurality, especially from a progressive point of view, can be seen as a positive codification and recognition of a diverse society at face value. Salvador Shavelson (2018) praises the relevance of the plurinational model emphasizing that it results from a postcolonial and experimental constitutionalism, which following a crisis of liberal democracy brings a 'demodiversity' that combines diverse expressions of democracy. The author stresses that people should retain the constituent power and its strength should not be taken by the constituted power.

Without ignoring its progressive attempt (and perhaps achievement), it is necessary to recognize that such plurality of 'the people' at the constitutional level runs the risk of evolving into a multiclass system in which a majority of citizens are excluded from the privileges granted to specially singled-out groups. This model, whereby different groups have different access to statehood, and where they may even construct their own statehood within the new plurinational State, could generate inequality before the law. In consequence, it has been argued that the omission of vast majorities for not belonging to singled-out groups is not compatible with a consistent system of rule of law (Lazarte 2015).

Constitutional procedures

Considering the Constitution's preamble, the 'how?' part of the questions referring to the means of rule, is also problematic. Preambles are often the introduction which sets the ideological tone for reading the legal text. The one at hand is quite telling. In it, colonialism is set next to republicanism and neoliberalism. Here the issue is how to construe the meaning of the following articles that are to form the basis for a stable democracy. Stable democratic principles are, however, inherently liberal and ultimately republican. The preamble, however, puts liberalism and republicanism as evils to be vanquished or condemned, just as colonialism. This is an openly political statement of purpose. Whereby liberalism conveys to the individual the freedom to self-determination within the protection and restraints of the rule of law, and republicanism simply encapsulates the principle of changing governments as opposed to monarchical succession, the drafters of the document seem to have had other evils in mind, or regretful memories from the past when leaving these principles behind for the constitution of the new plurinational State. The constructive wording comes when it also proposes to take the historic challenge to build a 'Unified Social State of Plurinational Communitarian law', which includes and articulates the goal of advancing toward a democratic, productive and peaceful Bolivia, committed to the full development and free determination of the people.

This intricate rhetoric has led to an inherent awkwardness in the constitution of the governmental organs, with contradictions and malfunctioning as the result. To illustrate '*how*' these organs (mis)rule, I shall analyze a few features of the legislative process and the judicial system.

The legislative process

A structural flaw of the State envisioned in the 2009 Constitution is the way in which the legislative branch is constituted and works. Legislative branches are the ones that take care of the '*what*', the body of law, i.e. the measures that have been taken to rule. Legislative power is where the rule of law meets the political representation of society. Legislators, elected by the people, discuss new laws, abrogate them or change them. Since laws are the basis upon the executive acts legitimately, they are the ultimate '*what*'.

In the first chapter of the second part of the Constitution the outlined structure of the Legislative focuses primarily on the position, rights and duties of the members of the chambers (Article 146–158), delineating its functioning only in three articles (Article 159–162). But a more poignant issue is found in Article 163. Here the initiative right for proposing legislation to the Legislative Assembly is given to basically everyone. Citizens, the parliamentarians themselves, the Executive organ, the Supreme Tribunal (in matter of judicial initiatives) and the autonomous governments can all initiate legislation. This wide range of sources of legislative initiative should provide for a more democratic debate and a more democratic deliberation of alternatives over concerns, bill projects and objectives. Unfortunately, the Bolivian legislative tradition, even before the new 2009 constitution, shows a different picture, one in which legislation approval is mostly associated with the Executive organ dictums. Disseminated sources of the legislative initiative also serve to undermine the power of fractions and the role of political parties as vehicles of consensus building. The legitimacy of elected members of the Legislative Assembly is certainly undisputed but it is, on its own, insufficient to provide good governance. As Pierre Rosanvallon (2009) explains, legitimacy in democracy comprises impartiality, reflexivity and proximity of actors and institutions. These virtues have historically not been characteristic of the Bolivian Legislative.

Traditionally the voting practice by the majority of legislators of the ruling party has provided undisputed backing to the executive. This practice of unconditional support in the Congress of the Republic has also continued after the promulgation of the new constitution, into the Plurinational Assembly. The MAS-IPSP party had a majority in both chambers throughout its rule. It even gained two-thirds of the bench at the 2009 and 2014 elections, obtaining the qualified majority needed for specific proceedings, such as presidential impeachment, ministerial interpellations or constitutional amendment procedures. This majority was mostly used in favor of the party's aims and rarely any dissent came from the representatives, rendering this branch of the State rather toothless during this period of time.

Adding to the weakness of the legislative branch is the expediency by which it can pass legislation. The passing of budgets is exemplary in this regard. Article 158.11 foresees the process by which the budget is to be passed. It sets a timeframe of 60 days after the executive presents its draft, after which, if it has not yet been approved, the project will be passed automatically. Considering that budgeting is one of the most fundamental of State duties, the lack of debate with which the executive can push for its draft to be passed is problematic, to say the least.

Another example of the weakness of the legislative branch is how it has failed to promote checks and balances by means of its right to interpellate cabinet ministers, as normed by Article 158 inc. 18. With a two-thirds majority, the Legislative Assembly can oust a minister following his or her censure. Yet in the last legislative periods under the MAS government, despite several interpellations made by opposition members of the Assembly, no minister was censured from the government by the MAS legislative majority. On the contrary, the ministers left with motions of approval, which has sown distrust and doubt, casting in a very bad light the independence and effective representation of constituencies by members of the Assembly. As a recent mockery, undermining the value of the Constitution and in open contempt of the Legislative Assembly, interim president Áñez restored three censured ministers (Erbol 2020).

Article 159, 12 provides that the lower chamber submits to the president shortlisted candidates for the appointment as heads of economic and social agencies and other positions in which the State participates by absolute majority. This provision of coordination between two powers is not effective either, as the positions are generally directly appointed by the president with the addition of 'interim', circumventing the parliamentary majority participation in their appointment.

This dysfunction between the organs of public power which according to article 12 of the Constitution are independent, separate and must coordinate and cooperate to fulfill their power, underlies the tendency to accumulate some circumstantially convenient attributions to the presidency. This lack of coordination between the legislative and the executive powers became even more evident in the recent transitional government. Perhaps the most explicit example is that of the ascension of Jeanine Áñez to the presidency in November 2019. The Constitution in its Article 161, 3. provides that the legislative chambers meet in a joint Assembly to admit or deny the resignation of the [resident or Vice-president of the State. This rule was omitted when the second Vice-president of the Senate, Jeanine Áñez, proclaimed herself president of the State in a session without a quorum and sheltered by officers of the Armed forces who imposed the presidential symbols on her. The Plurinational Constitutional Court issued a curious 'statement' endorsing this behavior with unsound arguments, violating the basic procedure that a Court must honor, i.e. a pronouncement must follow a process and not political urgency (El Universo 2019).

The judicial system

The next part of the question is the 'who does what', which is a simple way of asking who is the ruler and how do they rule. In a democracy, the ruler is 'the people', but obviously not directly. States have organs which administer power – mostly divided into three branches of government: the judicative, legislative, and executive. These for their part, are often chosen directly or indirectly by the people to rule on their behalf. The exercise to pinpoint exactly how and who rules in Bolivia reveals severe constitutional complexities.

The Bolivian judiciary is partitioned into the following jurisdictions: the ordinary jurisdiction headed by the Supreme Justice Tribunal, the agro-environmental jurisdiction headed by the Agro-environmental tribunal, the Rural, Native Indigenous Jurisdiction encompassing various legal systems and constitutional jurisdiction headed by the Constitutional Tribunal. This specific ailment of overlapping jurisdictions derives from the massive catalogue of rights that characterizes the 2009 Constitution. A unique aspect and so vast in scope, the catalogue is in itself a rich branch for analysis.[3] In an attempt at brevity, it can cautiously be summarized as a catalogue that seeks to delineate all the possible rights that could surge in the interactions of human beings with the State and with each other, insofar as the effects of the said interaction can be adjudicated, or somehow affected by the State. This maximalist catalogue of rights underlies the extensive overlap of jurisdictions that renders the judicial system inaccessible or ineffective. By its mere presence in the constitutional text, virtually every grievance can fall under the various jurisdictions available but ultimately under the Constitutional Court, creating the overlap which effectively undermines its role as the ultimate arbiter. Therefore, in the current Bolivian system, the ultimate judicial '*who*' is missing.

A comprehensive analysis of the judiciary would probably indicate the flaws of the constitutional design and its inadequate performance in delivering independent, reliable and expeditious justice to the people. After 11 years since the Constitution's renewal, the judicial system remains one of the main challenges pending review and reform (Orias and Idacochea 2020). I will briefly address three issues brought by the Constitution that call for special attention: legal pluralism, popular election of magistrates and judicial review of the constitution.

According to Article 1 of the Constitution, Bolivia is founded on plurality and on political, economic, juridical, cultural and linguistic pluralism. This concept brought 'legal pluralism' into a judicial system traditionally framed as unitary and centralized. The debate in Bolivia on the virtues or defects of this new founding principle has begun with inconveniences, and it will be prolonged as the transformation of a social, cultural, political and legal culture founded on traditional centralism and legal monism will not be easily achieved. It is not simple to admit that 'law' can have definitions so different from those that arise from liberal constitutionalism in the State. Nor will it be easy to preserve the plurality of the other systems or rights, without the risk of making these systems official and centralizing them through State recognition. As an example, in 2010 a demarcation law was enacted in order to define the limits of the jurisdiction for the indigenous justice system. The Constitutional Tribunal has expanded the 2010 Law's understanding through decisions that provide for an ample and progressive interpretation of the indigenous jurisdictions in order to assure their standing, recognition of pluractionality and the self-determination of indigenous, native and peasant people as a binding precedent (Tribunal Constitucional Plurinacional de Bolivia 2013).

The Constituent Assembly opted for the popular election of the magistrates as the best mechanism to guarantee their independence in the jurisdictional function. This modality is provided for in Article 182, 188 and 198 of the Constitution. After two elections, since it was enacted, the election of magistrates continues to be subject to severe criticism for its contradictory effect of turning judges into a sort of representative political authority. Voters connected the elected judges to the political majority at the Legislative Assembly that approved the shortlisted candidates, a majority that was held by the MAS-IPSP ruling party in both instances. This contradicts the liberal principle of independence of the judiciary, where judges do not represent anyone and should resolve their cases only according to the law (not to the opinion of their voters). Arguably, the appointment of judges should require a more precise scrutiny of the candidates than the current ballot popularity. Ultimately, the legitimacy that arises from the good performance of the judicial function is more important than the legitimacy of the origin of the mandate, as this is what, in the last analysis, will guarantee the true independence of judicial tribunals.

In the constitutional amendment process in the late 90s, Bolivia created a specialized Constitutional Court for judicial review and interpretation of the Constitution. The current Constitution in Article 196 provides for the establishment of the Plurinational Constitutional Court to assure the supremacy of the Constitution, to exercise constitutional control, and to safeguard constitutional rights and guarantees. This court has contributed importantly to the strengthening of the rule of law. Nonetheless, the institution has also been a victim of political instability and its destructive effects that rendered it inoperative in critical times, for example, during the constituent assembly or while issuing doubtful decisions regarding the reelection of authorities of the Executive office or their self-proclamation in office.

The Constitutional Court faces convolutions related to the nature and extent of the judicial review and interpretation of the Constitution. Its design followed flawed adaptations of foreign, mostly European, concentrated models. As a court in charge of ensuring the primacy of the Constitution through defense actions, it exerts a broad and diverse jurisdiction by reviewing cases generated in lower courts of all natures, becoming an ultimate space for judicial remedy. This broad scope of cases reaching the Constitutional Tribunal has created conflicts with other tribunals regarding the diverse understandings of precedents and their binding nature. Procedures and consultations on the constitutionality of legislative initiatives or executive orders have also become a space for delaying or blocking political disputes. Lacking a compulsory self-restraint statute, the Court cannot derive matters to other courts or public agencies to concentrate on strictly constitutional issues. As J.S. Elias (2011) argues, judicial review of constitutionality involves the displacement of the legislative majorities by the judicial majorities and it can be as fallible as that of other collective bodies but of less legitimacy from the democratic point of view. These and other ideas are being and should be debated to optimize such an important jurisdiction in Bolivia.

Crisis: a new constitutional moment

The ideological flavor, the absence of proper deliberation at the constituent convention and non-rigorous drafting created these constitutional inconveniences, which do not work properly. The constitution fails to determine many 'whos'. It is still unclear who oversees the legislative process and how legislation is to be implemented and by whom, or who is the arbiter of last resort in judicial matters. Even worse, the attempt at codifying plurality has confused the identity of who is to rule and in who's stead, thus creating a divided society. The question then, *who does what for whom?*, remains woefully unclear in the Bolivian constitution of 2009. However, there are ways ahead as well.

Severe crises recently shook Bolivia: devastating Amazon forest fires, electoral failures with political and social unrest and the uncontrolled COVID-19 pandemic. In each one it was found that the State, its institutions and its leaders were not prepared to face them properly, justifying the concerns of a society that expects a more efficient and reliable State. All these events open a constituent moment to transform the State and seek a new social pact based on positive experiences and lessons learned in recent times. There are many and very important issues that must be dealt with by the constituent power, which belongs only to the citizens. It's clear that far-reaching political agreements are indispensable to overcoming the current state of crisis. These are urgent ones, namely the pandemic as well as the current political and economic crises.

In my experience as interim president of Bolivia, I learned that timely and transparent elections were effective in renewing the organs of the State; yet this required structural agreements to be made between the main political actors and civil society in general. In 2005 negotiations paved the road for general elections, regional referendums, the election of local governors and a new constituent assembly. Free and fair elections were held and an orderly transition to a newly elected government took place. In contrast, the interim government of Áñez built an official narrative of disqualification of the MAS-IPSP party. It promoted judicial pursuits against its leaders, clearly neglecting its neutrality as a caretaker administration that was solely in charge of a new electoral process. Dialogue, coordination or cooperation amongst public organs or agencies was virtually non-existent.

Bolivians are facing one of the worst crises in our country's history. The pandemic has put everyone's life and health at risk, and we are still struggling to meet the minimum conditions necessary to face it. Schools and universities have closed their classrooms, virtual teaching exposes social inequality, as certain sectors lack access to the internet or any communicational technology. Our economy has been weakened to the point that we are dependent on external credit to cover current spending and our main sources of income, which sustains public interest, have been seriously affected. Public and private companies have reduced their activity dramatically or closed altogether. The dramatically slowed economy has increased unemployment, generated a labor crisis and spread poverty.

Instability and crisis are tackled by agreeing on pacts and sacrifices made for the greater good of a country. In the same way that citizens are obliged to attend elections, political leaders are obliged to offer society a minimum set of agreements that put political differences aside and offer measures to improve everyone's lives. These agreements must establish the basis for the rebuilding of the economy, education and judicial system. They must also kickstart a debate on how the country must be ruled from now onward. To put it briefly, this need for change and the settlement for basic agreements is a constitutional moment.

The constitutional derailment of 2019 and the 2020 elections, a new episode

As described above, key institutional issues are at the heart of the Bolivian governance equilibrium. They turned out to be woefully evident during the last 2019 political crisis and of unavoidable attention after the results of the 2020 election.

In praxis and in many ways the Bolivian constitution was ignored by the MAS party and the Morales administration to rule by formally legal but ultimately populist means. However, when the popular legitimacy of the Morales regime began to fade away, the institutions of the Plurinational State had no means to cope with the implosion of power at the executive's heart. The legislative branch was toothless, the electoral authority was not neutral and the judicial one was all but impartial and cohesive. Social upheaval seemed then the only way that political dissent could be aired. The MAS government, having relied more on the general public's approval than on the legitimacy enjoyed by rules-bound procedural government, crumbled as the people it supposedly represented turned against it.

The Constitution of 2009 often alludes to collectives, rather than individual rights in the points of political and stately participation (chiefly Article 3). Hereby the collectives, in other words, the masses, have outright constitutional legitimacy which makes them all-powerful, especially when defying all other non-popular actors within the State. An ever-growing distance between the government and society did not find a peaceful resolution in the referendum of 2016, where the government of Morales sought to circumvent the new constitution to grant him reelection. The MAS government sought legal means to subvert its defeat in the so-called 21 F referendum of 2016. In November 2017, the Constitutional Court granted a human right to reelection to all holders of public offices (Tribunal Constitucional Plurinacional de Bolivia, 2017). This allowed Mr. Morales to seek reelection in the 2019 elections, when his last mandate would have lapsed. This brazen decision by the Constitutional Court single-handedly broke down the legitimacy of the Constitution as a document of consensus. The hollowing out of Article 156, 168, 285 and 288 regulating national authorities' terms marked the end of the rule of abstract constitutional law over day-to-day political procedures. This way a door was opened for collective dissidence.

Neither the government at first, nor the people afterward felt fully bound by the 2009 constitution. Open conflict erupted as news of electoral fraud broke during a blackout at night on Election Day. As protestors took the streets and the international community started doubting the legitimacy of the vote, tensions intensified, to the eventual breakdown of peace. Disorder consumed the country as electoral precincts where ballots were held were burned. Compromise seemed possible, yet it did not break through. Ultimately, the rule of law, after a long erosion, was factually non-existent. Mob rule thus replaced the democratic government of Mr. Morales. Ochlocracy took hold of Bolivia after the 2019 elections. It is to be pointed out that, if one follows the liberal doctrine, that democracies primarily divide power into individual suffrage which is then stitched together by deliberation through the means of legislation and elections. In stark contrast, it can be argued that in Bolivia, the over-mighty and institutionalized presence of an overriding collective, or collectives, became destructive to democracy itself. Ultimately, collectives are different in their power than any democratic institution. Theirs is power emanating from an ephemeral yet absolute sense of belonging to a clear-cut cause. Collective power acts fast and is not bound to the outcomes of its exercise.

Democratic institutions, such as elected governments and legislative bodies are slow, deliberative, transparent and contradictory, as well as conciliatory. Democratic institutions, unlike the collectives, need the maximum number of voters to carry their decisions in order to be effective, as they rule by consent and not by dominance. This is the key issue in Bolivia. The institutions there never ruled fully as consent-seeking actors but as channels of collective dominance. Once these channels were severed, the collectives themselves rebelled on the streets against the institutions, and thus ended their rule.

Conclusion

In closing, this document recalls that elections took place in an orderly manner in October 2020. A record number of Bolivians went to the polls and elected the MAS-IPSP candidates for the presidency and vice-presidency with an outstanding majority of 55%, and members of the Legislative Assembly, where also they got an absolute majority. It is yet to be seen how the new rulers will conform and launch their government. But the key question relates to how the MAS-IPSP, as the leading political party will be able to promote and strike governance deals with the opposition on fundamental issues to tackle the current crisis and beyond. A common understanding of its severity and the lessons learned throughout the last year should be more compelling than mere demands for accountability and judicial pursuits.

Regrettably, at the time of writing, this promising return to democracy with renewed elected actors and institutions is being tainted again by ochlocratic forces. So-called civic leaders and citizen's platforms that oppose the MAS-IPSP party, from Santa Cruz, Cochabamba and Sucre launched mob demonstrations and strikes alleging electoral fraud; only days away from the presidential inauguration, it was rather baffling to note how protests at barracks and police stations demanded military rule. Those participating claimed to have defended democracy from Mr. Morales' rigging of elections in the previous year whilst calling for its end. This deep fissure needs to be healed. The method to do this is not to replace the government, but to change how it operates, so that grievances from all sides can be settled with basic agreements regarding common rules for the conduction of political competition.

On the basis of the presented analysis, it follows that Bolivia needs to seriously address the root of the recent multidimensional crises. The results of successful elections in 2020, including the praise of the newly elected authorities promising a more inclusive and reconciliatory government is a worthy signal for consensus building and for the reshaping of key democratic institutions in a new Constitution. It opens a genuine constitutional moment to renew a social pact, avoid disruptive pendulum effects and ensure sustainable peace.

Notes

1 According to the Supreme Electoral Tribunal official results: MAS, 55.11%, CC, 28, 83%, CREEMOS, 14,00% (OEP 2020).

2 Constitución Política del Estado, Texto Aprobado en Referéndum Constituyente de enero de 2009. Vicepresidencia del Estado Plurinacional de Bolivia, 2009. Article 172 provides for 27 tasks for the president of the State, along with others set by the Constitution and the law, p. 62.

3 Articles 13 to 107 provide for fundamental rights and guarantees, civil and political, of nations and rural native indigenous peoples, social and economic, environmental, health and social security, work and employment, property, of children and youth, of family, of elderly adults, of disabled persons, of persons deprived of liberty, of users of services and consumers, education, cultural diversity, science and technology and sports and recreation.

References

Coup d'etat Dataset (n.d.) https://www.jonathanmpowell.com/coup-detat-dataset.html

Crossman, R.H.S. (1966) 'Introduction by R.H. S. Crossman' in Bagehot, W. (ed) *The English Constitution.* Cornell University Press, New York.

El Universo (2019) 'Tribunal Constitucional de Bolivia avala a Jeanine Áñez como presidenta interina', 12 November. https://www.eluniverso.com/noticias/2019/11/12/nota/7601600/tribunal-constitucional-bolivia-avala-jeanine-anez-como-presidenta

Elias, J.S. (2011) 'Notas para pensar el control judicial de la constitucionalidad' in Gargarella, R. (ed) *La Constitución en 2020, 48 propuestas para una sociedad igualitaria.* Siglo Veintinuno XXI Editores, Buenos Aires.

Erbol (2020) 'Retornan Murillo y Cárdenas; Añez vuelve a posesionar a ministros censurados por la Asamblea', 20 October. https://erbol.com.bo/nacional/vuelven-murillo-y-c%C3%A1rdenas-a%C3%B1ez-vuelve-posesionar-ministros-censurados-por-la-asamblea

Gargarella, R. (ed) (2011) *La Constitución en 2020, 48 propuestas para una sociedad igualitaria.* Siglo Veintinuno XXI Editores, Buenos Aires.

Lazarte, J. (2015) *Reforma del 'experimento' constitucional en Bolivia. Claves de un nuevo modelo estatal y societal de derecho.* Plural editores, La Paz.

OEP Organo Electoral Plurinacional (2020) *Publicación de reulstados. Elecciones generales 2020.* 23 October. https://www.oep.org.bo/wp-content/uploads/2020/10/Separata_Resultados_EG_2020.pdf

Orias, R. and Indacochea, U. (2020) 'Bolivia: independencia judicial en la encrucijada', *Página Siete,* 2 October. https://www.paginasiete.bo/opinion/2020/10/2/bolivia-independencia-judicial-en-la-encrucijada-270046.html

Rodríguez Veltzé, E. (2008) 'The Development of Constituent Power in Bolivia' in Crabtree, J. and Whitehead, L. (eds) *Unresolved Tensions: BOLIVIA Past and Present.* University of Pittsburg Press, Pittsburg, pp. 145–159.

Rojas Tudela, F. (2018) *Constitución y Deconstrucción.* Vicepresidencia del Estado Plurinacional de Bolivia, Centro de Investigaciones Sociales, La Paz.

Rosanvallon, P. (2009) *La Legitimidad Democrática.* Manantial Editores, Buenos Aires.

Shavelson, S. (2018) 'Puede un silencio ser Constituyente?' in de Sousa Santos, B and Exeni Rodríguez, J.L. (eds) *Estado Plurinacional y Democracias.* Plural Editores, La Paz.

The New York Times (2005) 'New Bolivian Leader Bids to Quell Rifts', 10 June. https://www.nytimes.com/2005/06/10/world/americas/new-bolivian-leader-bids-to-quell-rifts.html

Tribunal Constitucional Plurinacional de Bolivia (2013) 'Sentencia Constitucional Plurinacional 0037/2013', 4 January. https://buscador.tcpbolivia.bo/_buscador/(S(jauqmf2xpgia2y3icl3wdd4o))/WfrFechaResolucion.aspx

Tribunal Constitucional Plurinacional de Bolivia (2017) 'Sentencia Constitucional Plurinacional 0084/2017, 28 November. https://buscador.tcpbolivia.bo/_buscador/(S(pkidhgn44h24hpwgpbx2j0gf))/WfrResoluciones1.aspx

2 Protest State and street politics

Bolivian social movements in the 2019–2020 crisis

Soledad Valdivia Rivera

Introduction

It is remarkable that the term of the first indigenous president of Bolivia would be both preceded and succeeded by a political crisis and a transitional government. Social movements ousted two presidents in 2003 and 2005, and their support was key in bringing Evo Morales to the presidential seat in 2005 as the leader of the Movement towards Socialism (MAS): at the time foremost 'the political instrument' of popular social movements. It was also amidst continued street protests demanding his resignation that Morales too was forcefully removed from power in November 2019. Large differences separate these historical events but they are evidential to the significant consequence of social movements in Bolivian politics. Indeed, the MAS government oversaw radical State transformations and social change directly linked to the demands by social movements, changes felt by vast sectors of society particularly in terms of wealth distribution and socio-political inclusion. This explains the high level of electoral support for the MAS party, having won the 2009 and 2014 national elections with over 60% votes. But even the overwhelming power at the institutional level, derived by its control of both the legislative assembly and the senate by two thirds from 2009, did not prevent social movements from pushing back against controversial governmental plans, destabilizing the administration and at times forcing it to step back. This chapter maintains that social movements have been and continue to be the most decisive actor in the Bolivian political process. For that reason, the State-social movements' relation is crucial to our understanding of the underlying developments that led up to the 2019–2020 crisis, as well as making sense of the baffling events of October/November 2019. This chapter traces the relation, paying particular attention to the rise of 'right wing' social movements in opposition to MAS, arguing that social movements have become a sine qua non, rendering any political force unable to govern without 'contentious power'.

The chapter's first part lays the theoretical ground for the analysis, discussing the role of social movements in a democratic political process and introducing the concept of 'protest State' for its explanatory power in the case of Bolivia. The following sections trace the development of the State-social movements' relation under the Morales administration. First, I discuss how the combination of the MAS' electoral success and the development of the social movement into the most legitimate vehicle of citizen representation and participation shaped the relation in a way that although effective in containing oppositional forces would gradually erode the bond between the MAS and its popular base of support. I then turn to the rise of oppositional social movements around old and new demands that grew stronger and more conflated towards the end of Morales' third term. In the last section I explain how these two developments set the stage for the fall of Morales, creating a window of opportunity of the failed election for oppositional forces to forcefully take over power with a certain level of legitimacy. In this part, I also discuss how the MAS and anti-MAS flanks evolved under the Áñez presidency, paving the way for the return of the MAS. The concluding section reflects on the importance of social movements for the political future of the country.

Democracy, social movements and 'protest State'

The question of democracy has been central to the public political debate, crystallized in the question of whether the fall of Morales in November 2019 was the result of a 'citizen revolution' or a 'coup'. Understood as a kind of relation between the State and society, one in which the first one acts mainly in response and conformity to the latter (Tilly 2007), there are roughly two positions concerning the role and effect of social movements for democratization: negative and positive. The State-social movements' relation is conceived as part of the interaction between citizens, social movements, the political party system and the State (Craig Jenkins and Klandermans 1995). On the one hand, the political party system ideally organizes and regulates access to State power by different groups in society (Mainwaring and Scully 1995). In consequence, strong social movements could not only be perceived as indications of a deficiency in the functioning of democratic institutions but they are also seen to undermine the political party system to the detriment of the consolidation of formal representative democracy. On the other hand, from a 'cultural politics' perspective, social movements have an important role in democratization as they question the 'political culture' that excludes and oppresses certain groups of society. This is expressed in the struggle to democratize the whole of society and not only the political regime, including the cultural practices that embody the social relations of exclusion and inequality (Calderón et al. 1992; Alvarez et al. 1998). Social movements would play an important role in pressuring and stimulating the political system to be more responsive to the needs of (segments of) the citizenry, not only democratizing the political system but the society at large.

Both stances position social movements in opposition to the State as the realm of institutional politics, which basically limits the types of State-social movement relation to two: repression or manipulation. This is the base preoccupation in the often-used analytical categories of 'autonomy' and 'co-optation' in the characterization of the relation. Social movements' autonomy is seen as necessary to counterbalance the alienation and authoritarianism from a presupposed elitist and repressive State (Steyn 2012). However, a more nuanced view sees a level of rapprochement as indispensable. Coy and Hadeen state that it is practically impossible to discern between cooperation and co-optation in situations of imbalance of power, but that social movements should aim to maintain a fluctuating position relating to State power (2005). In the same vein, Earle has suggested that social movements need to find a 'delicate balance' in order to maximize the benefits of collaboration while avoiding falling into co-optation (2013).

Particularly in the case of Bolivia, the characterization in terms of 'autonomy' and 'co-optation' seems too reductionist, obscuring its complexity. According to Goldstone (2013), the range of State-social movements' relations is much wider, especially if the heterogeneity within State institutions is acknowledged, rendering the frontier between 'institutionalized' and 'non-institutionalized' politics vague and permeable. This line of thought has found resonance in several studies that have looked at the elusive barriers separating social movements from political parties (Schönwälder 1997, Roberts 1998, Desai 2003, Glenn 2003, Deonandan and Close 2007, Van Cott 2005, 2008, Kitschelt 2006, Dufour 2008, Anria 2013). The various and varying relationships social movements maintain with political parties and the State could even ask for a different conceptualization of the phenomenon. As de Bakker, den Hond and Laarmanen (2017) show, more recently social movements have found new ways to organize, connect and enact collective action, particularly as a result of technological and communicational innovation, leading to more volatile forms of organizing. Although 'social movement' and 'social movement organization' retain elucidating value for the analysis, acknowledging the fluidity and continuity depending on the level of *organizing* as a process allows us to appreciate how that organizing process flows over the (analytical) borders that separate social movements (organizations), the State and political parties as distinctive entities.

Last, given the relatively high levels of social protest in the Latin American region, in a recent publication Moseley (2018) has proposed an innovative theoretical approach around the concept of 'protest State' that attains high explanatory power for the case of Bolivia. According to the author, the high levels of protest result from the dual process of political dysfunction and economic prosperity. Political dysfunction refers to the poor levels of performance of the State institutions that result in low levels of confidence. In parallel, the economic development has increased citizen awareness and organizational resources, producing a stronger and more engaged civil society. Moseley identifies four elements explaining the high levels of social protest: grievances, representation, repression and mobilizing structure. Grievances are necessary but not sufficient to trigger collective action. Too high levels of repression will inhibit social protest and so a minimum level of openness (democracy) is necessary. Moseley sees 'grievances' and 'repression' as fairly constant in Latin America, ascribing 'representation' and 'mobilizing structure' as the highest explanatory power. 'Representation' refers to the *promise* of viable vehicles of representation and its *failure* to deliver, whereas the mobilizing structure refers to the availability of organizational resources to citizens to engage in social protest. Where the political systems have become devoid of effective representative institutions, social protest becomes a conventional form of political participation for citizens, including the elite. As institutions remain weak, protest becomes a very likely option to a diversity of sectors in society. Interestingly, this is not limited to protest against the government, but also includes social mobilization in support of it. According to this author, in 'protest States' clientelist parties invest in building 'contentious power' by linking to organizations of civil society to enable and maintain street-based activism. In such scenarios, levels of protest remain high, regardless of the level of grievances.

On the basis of these theoretical considerations, in the remainder of the chapter, I trace the evolution of the State-social movement relation in recent years as key to the political process in Bolivia in general, and to the political crisis that started in October 2019, in particular. For the sake of clarity in the analysis, I will often refer to social movements (organizations) as 'actors', but I am building on its conceptualization as 'organizing processes' around specific issues. Also, the term *social movement* encompasses both popular (indigenous) social movements as well as the middle class, 'elite', 'right wing' or 'civic' social movements. This clarification is necessary as in the Bolivian public debate (and sometimes in the academic debate) the term social movement is almost 'exclusive' to the (indigenous) movements that form the base of support of the MAS.

The government of social movements

The end of military rule at the beginning of the 80s brought a period of increased tension between new social movements and the democratic State. In the 'lost decade' scenario of austerity and structural reforms, and in the face of rising levels of poverty and inequality, new social movements emerged in resistance to neoliberal policies. By the beginning of the 90s, it became evident that the double transition to democratic rule and a neoliberal model failed to deliver its promises of social and political inclusion, development and well-being to large sections of the population. The deficient functioning of political parties (Van Cott 2000, Mayorga 2004) rendered them unable to represent the growing discontent among popular sectors, pushing the articulation of social movements forward. The discontent derived into a double crisis of legitimacy of the political system and the neoliberal model marked by an intense period of social protest and mobilization between 2000 and 2005, with the Water War (2000) and the Gas War (2003) as the high points. Despite growing citizen disapproval, the governments of former dictator Hugo Bánzer Suarez and technocrat Gonzalo Sánchez de Lozada continued the implementation of a neoliberal agenda, including the privatization of natural resources enterprises. In this scenario, the people turned to the streets and social mobilization, leading to fatal clashes with the State and the reversal of governmental policies. The at-the-time president Sánchez de Lozada was even forced to resign and flee the country amidst the Gas War, and it would take little over a year before social protest would once again oust Carlos Mesa, his former vice-president, from the presidential seat.

The implications of the social outbursts were significant and manifold. First, it proved the efficiency of social movements as political actors and vehicles of citizen participation and representation. Second, it showed that it was possible to impose street politics, or 'contentious power', on the formal and institutionalized. Third, as a moment of deep political crisis, it made clear that profound reforms were necessary and imminent. And last, in the context of a legitimacy crisis of the political party system and the triumphant mood, social movements emerged as the legitimate actors to conduct the change. In a somewhat contradictory turn, the social movements opted to further unite electorally behind the charismatic leadership of Evo Morales and the MAS to participate in the December 2005 national elections. They defined the slogans of the political campaign, and after Morales was installed as president in January 2006, played an active role in the implementation of the political agenda they had set.

The 2005 electoral victory of Morales and MAS, with over 50% votes, constituted a turning point for the social movements. From then on, under the MAS government, social movements entered into a complex and fluctuating position by attempting to synergize institutional politics with 'contentious power', quite literally a 'government of social movements'. As if this was not challenging enough, the objective was nothing short of a revolution, the 're-foundation' of the Bolivian State to achieve radical social transformations, an objective that could count on the resistance from the politically displaced but still powerful economic elite.

The first years of the Morales government were marked by the confrontations around the Constituent Process. An original demand of the indigenous movement was that a new constitution was to be drafted by a Constituent Assembly. At first, the oppositional forces almost successfully sabotaged the assembly around procedural technicalities at the institutional level. The indigenous social movement organizations, coordinated under the umbrella entity Pacto de Unidad (Pact of Unity), organized vigils and social protests in response that were, in turn, met by mobilizations by the urban elite of the city of Sucre, where the Constituent Assembly was seated. While maintaining a firm foot on the streets, the indigenous movement drafted a complete proposal for the new Constitution pushing the process within the Assembly forward.[1] At that point, the resistance by the economic and displaced elites concentrated in the eastern region, where politicians sought to reinforce power at the local and regional political levels, mobilizing large segments of the urban population around the claim for regional autonomy, particularly in the region and city of Santa Cruz. The strong divide and confrontation even bordered on civil war, but the dual action of the social movements linked to MAS, both at the institutional space of the Assembly and the streets, defended the process and enabled its completion. The popular and indigenous pressure from the streets rescued the Assembly from complete stagnation, while the 'civic autonomous' movement was strong enough to force a few but very important concessions.[2] As I have argued before (Valdivia 2019), the discussions, confrontations and negotiations that took place in the realm of social movements were essential to the troubled constituent process and to shaping its result, demonstrating again the weight of non-institutional politics over the formal spaces of the State.

The promulgation of the 2009 Constitution was, to an extent, perceived as the defeat of the political opposition by the 'government of social movements'. The 2009 Constitution was approved by a referendum with 61% votes, and the elections held later that year yielded a 64% win for the party of Morales. The hegemonic position of the MAS appeased the conflicts with the political opposition that, from that moment, entered a period of fragmentation and loss of legitimacy, unable to articulate a plausible political discourse and project. At the same time, sustained economic growth and stability became markers of the Morales administration. The nationalization of the hydrocarbon sector in 2006 and the rising prices in the world market meant a considerable increase of the treasury while large parts started being redirected towards social policy. Until the end of the Morales administration, GDP averaged around 5% per year, GDP per capita doubled and poverty and inequality fell by half (Knaack 2020). The Bolivian 'economic wonder' was a source of legitimacy reinforcing MAS's hegemonic power. This is the stage of 'economic prosperity' that Moseley sees as the precondition for the rising levels of social protest that characterize the 'protest State'.

The two-thirds MAS majority in the legislative was crucial in shaping the relation of the State-social movements in the following years. Pro-indigenous policies and wealth redistribution amounted to unprecedented high levels of representation of many of the common and historical grievances, creating the space for contradictions and differences within MAS' plural coalition to surface. Social movement organizations moved back to sectorial demands amidst rising expectations generated by MAS hegemonic position and economic bonanza, leading to fragmentation and confrontation. The *Gasolinazo* conflict in 2010 and the TIPNIS-conflict in 2012 are most illustrative, where the MAS' absolute majority government was kept in check against these particular issues by quite 'autonomous' indigenous social protest (see also Valdivia 2019). However, when the political opposition and elite interests needed to be confronted, the popular support would again align sufficiently behind Morales, as illustrated by the electoral moments. Even the considerably destabilizing and delegitimizing

TIPNIS-conflict of 2012 did not prevent Morales from winning the 2014 national election, again with over 60% votes.

As I will explain below, the absolute MAS majority in the legislative practically neutralized the opposition at the institutional level, pushing it towards the domain of non-institutionalized politics where it adopted a strategy of destabilization and discrediting of the MAS government. This struggle took place to a large extent in the arena of the (social) media and the NGO-sector, explaining the hostilities under the Morales administration, but also through social protest. To confront this, most notably in the context of weak institutions, the MAS government turned to the social movements as a source of legitimacy and 'contentious power'. In a personal interview in January 2020 with the National Director of NINA, a decade-long program working on the construction of indigenous leadership (previously headed by the current vice-president David Choquehuanca), Walter Limache explained that instead of being the instrument of social movements, the social movements had become instrumental to MAS. The two-thirds majority rendered consultation unnecessary. Instead of social movements' demands and proposals flowing through MAS to the legislative, the decisions would be made at the high levels of the executive branch, reducing the social movements to an endorsing function (Limache, personal communication, La Paz January 2020; see also Farthing 2019 and Zuazo 2010). Clientelist and favouritism practices served to oil this gear wheel but did not prevent fissures and divisions as the effect of postponed demands. This modus operandus, although effective in containing oppositional forces, gradually eroded the relation between the MAS and its social base. Undermined support later would help create the window of opportunity to remove the MAS from power.

This erosion occurred in two dimensions: in State-social movement relation and within the social movement as an organizing process. The relative weight and equivocal position of the social movements conferred them a singular role in Bolivian politics that escapes the analytical dichotomy 'autonomy vs. co-optation'. Accusations of manipulative and co-opting practices addressed to the MAS government have been recurrent, both in the public and academic debates (Regalsky 2010, Anria 2013, McKay et al. 2014, Hollender 2016, Farthing 2019). The endorsing function arguably led to a gradual deterioration of the capacity of social movements for proposal to and interpellation of the MAS leadership (Limache, personal communication, La Paz January 2020). Within the social movements' organizations, the leadership changed. Decades of struggle against the State had produced committed and experienced leaderships that went quickly to occupy all sorts of political posts as MAS arrived to power. In the following years, MAS presence grew within the political institutions as the public sector expanded. The leadership of social movements' organizations was soon perceived as a bridge towards jobs in the public sector. According to Limache, the younger leaders had less experience and were no longer formed in the struggle against the political power but in collaboration with it, resulting in a lower 'historical consciousness' and lower commitment (personal communication, La Paz January 2020). As the State absorbed them, the leadership of the social movements' organizations became weaker and prone to internal fragmentations. This explains in part the emergence of parallel leadership structures, some promoted by the MAS government, in alignment and opposition to the MAS government (see for example Achtenberg, 2015), signalling the fragmentation and weakening of the social movements' *organizations*.

Notwithstanding, social movements may be more adequately conceptualized as organizing *processes*. From this perspective, the putative 'co-optation' could also be seen as the cooperative organizing process that flows over the (analytical) borders separating the social movement from other actors. In other words, the organizing processes around specific issues underlying the social movements' relation to the State show varying levels of oscillation between support and cooperation, and rejection and confrontation. In a situation in which the more profound shared grievances of the popular sectors had attained its historically highest level of representation at the institutional domain but were still under continuous siege by oppositional forces, the perceived urgency and risk of sectorial demands varied, resulting in divergent organizing processes around those demands. The 'co-optation' by the MAS government focuses on the social movements' *organizations, structure and leadership*, producing a characterization as weak, divided and subjugated. In doing so, it does not recognize the agency of their constituencies (as if they were sheep), and overlooks the fact that the dynamic and strategic calculations vary widely from when the social movement is outside the State and in open conflict with it, to when it enacts a much more complex and contradictory fluidity (as a process) transiting between institutional politics and street politics. From this perspective, the academic signalling of 'co-optation' and 'autonomy' appears too reductionist, while those in the public debate denote a mere political position.

In addition, structural institutional frailty and corruption gradually damaged the image of the MAS 'social movements' government. It must be noted that institutional weakness was not always detrimental to the Morales government as it, for better or for worse, allowed for a greater space of manoeuvre to the MAS charismatic leadership (see Van Cott 2008) and also for the social movements. According to Balderacchi (2017), the informal incorporation of social movements, resulting from weak institutions in Bolivia, permitted them to wield greater influence on the political process in comparison to the experiences of Ecuador and Venezuela. And this applied to social movements both in support and in opposition to the government.

Notwithstanding the multiple and changing forms that the social movement relation with the State can and did take, it remained the icon of legitimate political representation and participation. Amidst a dysfunctional political party system, the social movements emerged as the authentic and effective actors defining the political process in the period 2000–2005. Building and depending on this contentious power, the MAS discourse reinforced the narrative that social movements were politically virtuous, expressing the will of the people and as the true channels of citizen participation. With this narrative, MAS, first as the 'instrument' and later as the 'government' of social movements, was relatively successful in monopolizing its political capital. But it was precisely this discourse that made the MAS government very vulnerable to social movements that opposed it.

The rise of anti-MAS social movements

In an article of 2011, Salman pointed to the necessity to consider the development of 'opposition movements' in Bolivia, as 'social movement' seemed always to involve support for the government. The constituent process had seen the rise of opposition social movements around elite regionalist demands. In the years to come, the political opposition stood weak, unarticulated and prevented from any meaningful influence at the institutional level before the two-thirds MAS majority, and turned to 'street politics' as means of political participation. In that process, it would expand to include new faces and grievances. In his study of 'the process of change', Goodale dedicates a full, comprehensive and elucidating chapter to an ethnography of the opposition (2020). He shows that although 'conservative', 'economic' and 'regional' are salient characteristics, the opposition constitutes 'a nonlinear process deeply embedded in and shaped by Bolivia's distinct regional mytho-histories' incorporating 'multiple, competing, and alternative' national projects (p. 97). The contribution of Angus McNelly to this volume also offers an insightful account of the development of the regional autonomy movement as political-economic 'socio-historic bloc' that builds on transient processes of class alliances.

This multidimensional resistance to the MAS found an influential expression in social protest. In line with the conceptualization of social movements as an organizing process, these movements encompass a plurality of grievances, demands and actors, with the vague common denominator of being 'anti-MAS'. Although they condensed in the slogan 'Morales' resignation and democracy' amidst the alleged electoral fraud, the reasons behind the widespread social protests in November 2019 were more complex. I differentiate between a set of grievances of more legitimate nature around issues of democracy and the less legitimate vested interests.

Building on the theoretical tenets of 'protest State', the rise of these social movements in the first category answers to the combination of insufficient representation and increasing resource mobilization. The 'democratic' demands reflect the promises and high expectations that were generated by the 'government of social movements' and the 'indigenous State' (Postero 2017) in relation to its relative (and realistic) capacity to fulfil them. The economic bonanza under the Morales administration played a double role in this regard. It inflated the otherwise accurate perception that the State went through a period of unprecedented growth and institutional strength, and it increased the citizen's access to resources to become aware and mobilize around demands. A significant example of this is the launch of Bolivia's own telecommunication satellite Tupac Katari in 2013, that extended communication and internet services to remote populations while making it widely accessible by reducing consumer costs.

A first set of 'democratic' grievances reflect the local resistance to the implementation of large infrastructural and neo-extractivist projects that were perceived as the betrayal of the State discourse of defence of indigenous rights and the rights of Mother Earth. The TIPNIS-conflict is emblematic. The governmental plan to build a highway through a protected area and indigenous territory mobilized the local indigenous population, under the leadership of Fernando Vargas, around 'essentialised meanings of indigenous identity … to attain legitimacy for historical claims to territorial and political rights' (Perreault and Green 2013).[3] It was soon joined by the leader of the Confederación de los Pueblos Indígenas del Oriente Boliviano, Confederation of the Indigenous Peoples of Eastern Bolivia (CIDOB), a painful dissension at the social movement base of support of MAS. The movement achieved nationwide attention and support thanks to extensive although politicized media coverage,[4] expanding social protest under a plurality of actors, such as urban youngsters, ecologists, feminists, Indianists and cultural activists (Rivera Cusicanqui 2015).

This reflects the increased resources of the citizenry to become aware and mobilize around demands. In addition, cognizant of the destabilizing and delegitimizing effect of the conflict, the political opposition moved quickly to support the movement, illustrated by the unlikely alliance between Adolfo Chávez with Santa Cruz opposition leader Ruben Costas, who in 2008 had supported an illegal autonomy referendum with an extremely racist content. In the 2014 elections, the fraction of CIDOB headed by Chávez supported Costas' *Movimiento Demócrata Social* (MDS) (Social Democrat Movement), the parallel fraction headed by Melva Hurtado supported MAS, Fernando Vargas was the presidential ticket of opposition alliance Green Party, and indigenous CONAMAQ leading representative Rafael Quispe, having broken with MAS over this conflict, allied with the Frente de Unidad Nacional (National Unity Front) pertaining to businessman Samuel Doria Medina. Aside from the 'autonomy vs. co-optation' discussion, the social movement as an organizing process was successful in its aim to stop the construction of the highway.

Another example is the mobilizations headed by the *Comité Cívico Potosinista* (COMCIPO) (Civic Committee of Potosí) in 2010, 2015 and 2019. One of the poorest provinces of Bolivia, and in line with its colonial past, the economic activity of Potosí heavily depends on external actors: the demand for minerals and international tourism. During the first years of the Morales administration, the mining sector experienced an upturn due to the swelling global demand, leading to increased exploitation by transnationals in the mines of San Cristóbal and San Bartolomé, and posing a serious threat to the local communities' access to water. As the development of the province lagged behind, the sense of undelivered promises turned into political dissatisfaction erupting into weeks-long strikes in 2010 and 2015. The demands were chiefly material in nature, including unfulfilled promises of constructing hospitals, an airport and land reform, next to an increase of the benefits of the exports of resources for the region. On a deeper level, they reflected the perceived failure of the MAS government to radically transform the country's economy, maintaining its dependence on the export of raw natural resources and foreign capital investment, a sentiment shared by the local youth that otherwise supported the MAS (Colectivo Lucha de Clases 2017). In both stances, the slogan of regional autonomy resurfaced. By July 2019, in the run-up to the national election, under the leadership of Marco Antonio Pumari, COMCIPO joined other regional civic committees demanding that Morales decline his candidature. Pumari's national profile increased when he led another COMCIPO strike weeks before the election, demanding the annulment of the joint venture between the government and the German firm ACI for the exploitation and industrialization of lithium. The mobilization claimed that the conditions were detrimental to the Potosí province and its population. These soon conflated with the ones alleging electoral fraud and demanding Morales' resignation following the October 2019 election, catapulting Pumari to the national stage as one of the leaders of the general upsurge. Morales eventually dissolved the joint venture in early November, probably in the hope to appease the COMCIPO movement against him, proving once again the effectiveness of the social movement in Bolivia.

A second set of 'democratic' grievances revolved around the state of democracy in Bolivia, pointing more specifically to the poor performance of State institutions and its deterioration into an authoritarian regime. Corruption was a recurring theme as many cases were brought to light and were widely disseminated by media outlets. The Indigenous Fund case, involving funds aimed for the development of indigenous peoples and implicating social movement organizations' leadership and State authorities, was particularly painful. Although admitted by the government, the slow progress of the judicial process resulting in low convictions, discredited the MAS administration as another sign of arbitrary use of the judiciary. The government's attempts to reform and 'democratise' the traditionally weak judiciary system with elected judges were perceived as a move towards undermining its independence from the executive power.

'Democratic' grievances also developed around Morales' fourth candidature. Interviews held shortly after the election in October 2019 and in January 2020 with a variety of actors, including MAS members and supporters, former public authorities and members of the anti-MAS *Pititas* movement, coincided that the 21 February 2016 referendum constituted an inflexion point. At Morales' first defeat at the ballots since 2002, a thin majority of Bolivians voted against a constitutional reform that would allow him to run for president for the fourth consecutive time. During the period leading up to the referendum, the political opposition successfully pitched the NO campaign in the media as a 'citizen mobilization', finding resonance far beyond the traditional opposition of the urban upper classes. It appealed to new segments of the middle class, particularly the so-called 'Evo generation' youngsters who had come of age during a period of economic stability and growth as well as of significant reduction of poverty and inequality, and that would cast a vote for the first time in 2016 and 2019. As Achtenberg pointed out (2016), the MAS discourse of transformation and revolution gradually changed into one of pragmatism and stability that could not fully appeal to the youth's aspirations. To many of them, the elongated presidency of Evo Morales, the only one they could remember, appeared indeed as a sign of deterioration of democracy. The political fatigue of the relation with its social base after more than a decade in government was also reflected in the NO campaign support by dissidents of MAS. Detracting union and social leaders articulated severe criticism against Morales, accusing him of bringing the country further down the road of authoritarianism. These sentiments were confirmed to some and further spread to others when a ruling by the Constitutional Court allowed the fourth candidature of Morales in November 2017.

The successful attempt by the MAS administration to bypass the results of the '21F' incited a new social movement in defence of democracy around the slogans *Bolivia dijo NO* (Bolivia said NO) and *Mi voto se respeta* (My vote must be respected). In the months previous to the Constitutional Court ruling, the movement mobilized thousands of people in different cities of the country. By this time, it had become clear that the working class and indigenous face of social protest had found a new subject in the (new) middle class, wealthy and 'white'. Although at the level of formal politics the issue was settled within the margins of the law, the consecutive mobilizations both against and in favour of the Morales candidature demonstrated that the issue still needed to be settled at the level of street politics, with the important detail that it concerned an issue capable of unifying the opposition. As the 2019 elections moved closer, rallies continued. Despite the fact that most polls previous to the election showed Morales as the favoured choice, or perhaps because of it, eventually the discourse around the alleged authoritarianism and lack of legitimacy of his candidature started to be transferred to the electoral process, questioning the independence of the electoral court, and warning against an upcoming electoral fraud. Here too was the movement successful as this suspicion was amplified by (social) media to become a widespread belief: by September 2019 68% of the population believed electoral fraud would occur (Página Siete 2019).

A third strand of resistance emanates from the vested interests of an economic elite displaced from political power, accounting for the more elitist, racist and classist face of the opposition that sees the MAS 'process of change' as the loss of privilege and position in Bolivian society (see Goodale 2020). These grievances heartened mobilizations around the slogan of autonomy during the constituent period, with severe expressions of racist violence leading eventually to its decline (Gustafson 2009, Farthing 2019, Valdivia 2019). Its most recent articulation is found in the ultra-right-wing *Comité Cívico Pro-Santa Cruz* (Pro-Santa Cruz Civic Committee). It represents the Santa Cruz elite that consolidated first as approximately 40 families during the rubber boom to later include large landowners as the region became the largest agricultural exporter (Farthing, 2019), also connected to foreign, predominantly Brazilian, capital (Mckay 2020). After 2009, a series of agreements between the MAS government and the agro-business served to appease resistance, creating a 'State-capital alliance' that favoured the agro-business interests while reassuring MAS of its political power (Mckay 2020). They turned out to be but a truce in a struggle to maintain and regain political power tainted by regional, racists and classist sentiments. The Comité engrossed the '21F' and 'Bolivia dijo NO' movements and catapulted the leadership of Luis Fernando Camacho to the national stage. Days before the election in a multitude *cabildo* (rally), Camacho claimed that electoral fraud would occur and called for civilian disobedience in the event of a MAS victory while flagging federalism (Correo del Sur 2019). He led the mobilizations in the eastern region after the 2019 election, staging a dramatic delivery of Morales' letter of resignation and return of the bible to the governmental palace (Infobae 2019), as well as playing a dubious role in the events leading to the ascension of Jeanine Áñez to the presidency (Pando 2020). Later, he bragged about his father's role in convincing the police and military to turn against Morales (Erbol 2019).

The fall of Morales and the Añez government

The so-called '*Pititas*' (Little Ropes)[5] movement denotes the continuation of the social protest that preceded the 2019 election, in which the above-sketched demands conflated around the claim of electoral fraud and Morales' resignation. The movement constitutes the result of chiefly mid-term accumulation of grievances that found increased expression in the form of social movements. By means of social protest, it advanced and sustained the narrative of abuse of power and electoral fraud, genuinely believing it was enacting the recuperation of democracy. The roles of Carlos Mesa, Luis Fernando Camacho, the police, the military and the preliminary report of the OAS audit were more decisive to the fall of Morales. However, the 'Pititas', by the validity and authenticity inferred to the social movement format, was key in legitimizing the events that advanced and consolidated Áñez in power amidst the weakened 'contentious power' of the MAS.

Thus, after its decline in 2009, the opposition experienced a recovery and re-composition around old and new grievances. It evolved into a political network (Kenis and Schneider 1991, Börzel 1997, Bogason and Musso 2006) that brought together a variety of actors behind a common goal, mirroring the political network conformed by MAS behind the political project of 'the process of change' (Valdivia 2019). Both show the gearing of actors and processes across the domains of institutional politics and street politics. As an example, in the run-up to the 2019 elections, the political alliance *Bolivia dice NO* (Bolivia says NO) was created in a very literal attempt to connect the *Bolivia dijo NO* movement to political parties. In the same vein, Carlos Mesa's Comunidad Ciudadana also coordinated political parties and other civil society movements called *plataformas ciudadanas* (citizen platforms) into an electoral option. The internal differences prevented the creation of a single anti-MAS electoral front. But the very specific aim to topple Morales (not even MAS) intensified the mobilization of resources and actors as it became clear that this would not be achieved by electoral means, successfully unifying in social protest behind that common objective.[6] Thus, the October and November 2019 events display the clash between these two large political networks, transiting between institutionalized and street politics and overflowing borders, where the one lead by the oppositional forces obviously got the upper hand. The social protest was crucial in installing and reinforcing the narrative of the electoral fraud, while inferring legitimacy and investing a veil of 'lawfulness' to political processes and moves which, certainly in retrospect, can be rightly characterized as coup d'état.

If the October and November 2019 events leading to Jeanine Áñez's presidency remain confusing or controversial to some – in regard to whether or not a coup took place – the blatant undemocratic performance of her administration has left little room for discussion. From the beginning it was made clear that the Áñez government, far from its formal role as caretaker, set out to reverse the political course of the previous government (Wolf 2020), overtly exceeding its mandate by means of an authoritarian crackdown on racist violence (Farthing 2020). The human rights violations and political persecutions have been widely denounced and reported, including reports by the International Human Rights Clinic (2020), Human Rights Watch (2020), the UN Office of the High Commissioner for Human Rights (2020) and the Inter-American Commission for Human Rights (2020). The 'pacification' in November 2019 came at the cost of at least 22 deaths of protesters who were massacred by the military in the locations of Sacaba and Senkata. After that, in the words of Stefanoni (2020) 'revanchism won out over institutionalism, repression over inclusion, and the chaotic and deficient new administration was quickly overwhelmed by the crisis generated by Covid-19…' In addition, flagrant corruption scandals accompanied with impunity have marked the Áñez administration (Página Siete 2020), featuring the governmental acquisition of 170 highly overprized ventilators to attend COVID-19 patients that proved useless upon arrival (Miranda 2020). This has led outspoken critics Morales as Pablo Solón (2020) and María Galindo (2020), to characterize the Áñez administration as 'the worst government ever' after the bloody dictatorship of Luis García Meza.

The Áñez government presented an effort to recover the political power by a displaced oligarchic economic elite (Stefanoni 2020), with a clear expression in the (agro-) business elite of the Santa Cruz region (see also the contribution of Bret Gustafson to this volume) that, as soon as it took over, revealed the same vices it had denoted during the 90s, this time as right-wing populism (Molina 2020). It can be argued that the legitimate social movements that revolved around issues of democracy were co-opted or instrumentalized by the radical right-wing linked to vested interests, although in consequence with my own analysis, this is more a political opinion or too simplistic an academic inference. However, it is a fact that once the common objective of removing Morales from power was achieved, the political network started to disintegrate. This is reflected in the fragmentations within the institutional domain of the government and in the distancing of those sectors of society that gradually saw the betrayal of the democratic grievances for which they had mobilized. The high expectation of the restoration of democracy, efficiency and reconciliation were met with quite the opposite, leading to many frustrated citizens to opt for the MAS in the 2020 elections (Peñaranda 2020).

In 2020, the alliances between different sectors and actors of society as two opposed political networks reflected in the competing narratives 'fraud vs. coup', went through inverse processes. As the right-wing political network deteriorated and fragmented, the MAS political network with a core of social movements recuperated and unified amidst political repression and siege. This happened at the level of institutional politics in the MAS majority Assembly under the leadership of Eva Copa, but perhaps, more importantly, at the level of the streets. The salient image being the ten days nationwide blockade at the end of July 2020, staged by the base of support of MAS that imposed the immovable election date of 18 October and terminated the uncertainty of the electoral moment. The dissimilar developments reflect a qualitative difference between the two political networks. The organizational structures supporting the popular movements – -e.g. the indigenous social movement organizations conforming to Pacto de

Unidad, the *Central Obrera Bolivia* (COB) (Bolivian Workers Center), the Coca growers confederations, etc. – are the historical result of decades-long struggles, with a more 'organic', 'grass root' and consolidated nature. These have forged the longer perspective project of 'the process of change' that forms a common base of political articulation providing a stronger and notably more resilient substance to MAS. In comparison, the right-wing coalitions have proved more circumstantial and brittle. To see this, one needs but to take a quick look at the less than one year in power of the right-wing where the State was (legally and illegally) put in service of vested interests, leaving many of the demands around democracy (literally) postponed. The fractures in the right-wing government have been much deeper as expressed in the many episodes of conflict, contradiction and crisis within the executive power (Opinión 2020). Its weak substance is further demonstrated by the fact that even the electoral moment and the imminent MAS victory did not produce an alliance behind one candidature, let alone a unifying political proposal for the 2020 elections.[7] Its political project added to nothing more than the fall of Morales and the MAS, and even when it became clear these were not one and the same, it remained unable to articulate anything more than a rejection of MAS.

Conclusion

The results of the 2020 elections presuppose a continuation of the MAS political project: 'the process of change'. However, the MAS returns to the government under very different leadership and before a very different and complicated scenario. For the first time it will have to govern in austerity, while trying to emerge from a multidimensional crisis marked still by much uncertainty. Polarization may lose some of its instrumental value in the post-election scenario, but it is clear that long and mid-term social incisions have been deepened in an already fragmented society. Even before Luis Arce was installed, protests had already taken place. Some of these were staged before the barracks supplicating for a military government, indicating the extremism of some positions.

A powerful economic elite resents having been once again displaced from power and has demonstrated to be willing to use any means available to regain it. The (upper) middle-class democratic grievances are likely to continue under the new MAS leadership. They both have incorporated street politics. In addition, the Covid-19 crisis is bringing and will continue to bring increasing economic and social pressure, particularly to the constituencies of the MAS that, after the transition, demand restitution and compliance of 'their' government. Luis Arce has expressed the aim to lead a unifying and conciliatory government, but it remains to be seen how these centrifugal forces will be integrated, or at least contained.

The deteriorating economic situation may reduce organizational resources to some, but will aggravate grievances to most. In the context of weak representative institutions, social protest will continue as an effective form of citizen participation while the 2019–2020 crisis shows that this can come at a high cost, turning the political process belligerent and polarized. The new government will need to find ways to deal with it. The Morales government received wide criticism for weakening popular social movements by means of authoritarian, populist and co-optative practices. Even if the weaker structuration and articulation could be linked to higher levels of representativeness in State institutions (Moseley 2018), the surfacing of old and new grievances is to be expected in Bolivia's 'protest State'. Although social movements are not on their own sufficient or all-determining, institutional politics are vulnerable to social protest, and so it seems that no political force will be able to govern without sufficient 'contentious power'. So much have we learned from the Morales government. Since there is no register for incorporating social movements in the political process, we are bound to the experiment, improvisation and mistake. The question is if both State institutions and political actors, including the social movements, can learn and improve.

It must also be noted that deficient institutions are not the whole story. The plurality and diversity, and the historical schisms that characterize Bolivian society make you wonder of the possibility of a system able to capture it all. Hence the 'transits' and 'overflows' between State and society, for which social movements appear to be key. Attaining a certain balance between institutionalized and non-institutionalized politics seems to be necessary. This remains a challenge ahead.

Notes

1 The social movements organizations organized a series of consultation and deliberative events throughout the country. With the aid of national NGO's, they collected grass roots proposals and integrated them into one complete draft proposal (see also Garcés et al. 2010).

2 The concessions related to land reform were perceived as a betrayal by many MAS constituents, and remained a recurrent point of critique of MAS failure to address structural sources of exclusion and subjugation.

3 See also Lucero (2008), Fabricant (2012), McNeish (2013), Burman (2014), Canessa (2014), Laing (2015), Postero (2017), Fabricant and Postero (2015), Valdivia (2019).

4 The growing influence of the media in politics and its use as a political instrument is a widespread phenomenon (see for example Kitzberger 2010, 2012) also in Bolivia (Exeni 2010, ONADEM 2011). In the Latin American region, the media traditionally maintains close links to political elites (Fox, 1988). In the case of Bolivia, an outdated media law – the Print Law of 1925 – serves as a carte blanche for a media sector dominated by private-commercial actors and in the absence of public media (Exeni 2010). Attempts to reform the Print Law by the Morales administration have been met with resistance by the sector amidst accusations of censorship (see also Lupien 2013 and Valdivia 2019).

5 The name resulted from Morales' disdainful reference to the little ropes the mobilized middle- and upper-class citizens had to span over the streets of their neighbourhoods, as they were unable to man all blockades.

6 This characterization appears to correspond with the result of the 2020 election. Indigenous and democratic demands, after Áñez, seem better guarded by MAS in the eyes of in 2019 dissident indigenous and (lower middle class), illustrated by its increase from 47% to 55%. The democratic upper middle class and elite demands are represented by 30% of Comunidad Ciudadana. The 14% of Luis Fernando Camacho's Creemos, represents the radical populist right-wing minority of above all (agro-business) elite economic interests that build on historical regional sentiments.

7 It has been difficult for the opposition to compete with MAS policy in terms of content, particularly due to the MAS government's economic success. That explains why the political campaign has concentrated in character attacks, particularly on the address of Morales.

References

Achtenberg, E. (2015) 'A Vote for Local Democracy in Bolivia's Regional Elections', *NACLA*, 17 April. https://nacla.org/blog/2015/04/17/vote-local-democracy-bolivia%27s-regional-elections

Achtenberg, E. (2016) 'After the Referendum, What's Next For Bolivia's Progressive Left?', *NACLA*, 15 April. https://nacla.org/blog/2016/04/15/after-referendum-what%E2%80%99s-next-bolivia%E2%80%99s-progressive-left

Alvarez, S. et al. (1998) *Cultures of Politics and Politics of Cultures*. Westview Press, Boulder.

Anria, S. (2013) 'Social Movements, Party Organization and Populism: Insights from the Bolivian MAS', *Latin American Politics and Society*, vol 55, no 3, pp19–46.

Balderacchi, C. (2017) 'Participatory Mechanisms in Bolivia, Ecuador and Venezuela: Deepening or Undermining Democracy', *Government and Opposition*, vol 52, no 1, pp131–161.

Bogason, P. and Musso, J.A. (2006) 'The Democratic Prospects of Network Governance', *American Review of Public Administration*, vol 36, no 1, pp3–18.

Börzel, T.A. (1997) 'What's So Special about Policy Networks? – An Exploration of the Concept and Its Usefulness in Studying European Governance', *European Integration online Papers (EIoP)*, vol 1, no 16. http://eiop.or.at/eiop/texte/1997-016a.htm

Burman, A. (2014) '"Now We Are Indígenas": Hegemony and Indigeneity in the Bolivian Andes', *Latin American and Caribbean Ethnic Studies*, vol 9, no 3, pp247–271.

Calderón, F. et al. (1992) 'Social Movements: Actors, Theories, Expectations' in Escobar, A. et al. (eds) *The Making of Social Movements in Latin America: Identity, Strategy and Democracy*. Westview Press, Boulder.

Canessa, A. (2014) 'Conflict, Claim and Contradiction in the New Indigenous State of Bolivia', *Critique of Anthropology*, vol 34, no 2, pp151–171.

Colectivo Lucha de Clases (2017) 'El paro cívico de Potosí: la victoria del pueblo y el engaño regionalista'. 17 August. https://www.luchadeclases.org.bo/paro-civico-potosi/

Correo del Sur (2019) 'Cabildo llama a controlar elecciones y la desobediencia en caso de fraude', 4 October. https://correodelsur.com/politica/20191004_cabildo-llama-a-controlar-elecciones-y-la-desobediencia-en-caso-de-fraude.html

Coy, P.G. and Hedeen, T. (2005) 'A Stage Model of Social Movement Co-optation: Community Mediation in the United States', *The Sociological Quarterly*, vol 46, pp405–435.

Craig Jenkins, J. and Klandermans, B. (1995) *The Politics of Social Protest*. University of Minnesota Press, Minneapolis.

De Bakker, F.G.A., den Hond, F. and Laarmanen, M. (2017) 'Social Movements: Organization and Organizing' in C. Roggeband and B. Klandermans (eds) *Handbook of Social Movements across Disciplines*. Springer, New York.

Deonandan, K. and Close, D. (eds) (2007) *From Revolutionary Movements to Political Parties*. Palgrave Macmillan, New York.

Desai, M. (2003) 'From Movement to Party to Government. Why Social Policies in Kerala and West Bengal Are So Different' in Goldstone, J.A. (ed) *States, Parties and Social Movements*. Cambridge University Press, Cambridge.

Dufuour, P. (2008) 'From Protest to Partisan Politics: When and How Collective Actors Cross the Line', *Canadian Journal of Sociology*, vol 34, no 1, pp55–81.

Earle, L. (2013) 'Drawing the Line between State and Society: Social Movements, Participation and Autonomy in Brazil', *The Journal of Development Studies*, vol 49, no 1, pp56–71.

Erbol (2019) 'Camacho revela que su padre cerró con militares y policías para la renuncia de Evo', 28 December. https://erbol.com.bo/nacional/camacho-revela-que-su-padre-cerr%C3%B3-con-militares-y-polic%C3%ADas-para-la-renuncia-de-evo

Exeni, J.L. (2010) *Mediocracia de alta intensidad. Bolivia: Medios de comunicación y democracia en contextos de cambio*. Instituto Internacional para la Democracia y la Asistencia Electoral IDEA, La Paz.

Fabricant, N. (2012) *Mobilizing Bolivia's Displaced: Indigenous Politics and the Struggle over Land.* University of North Carolina Press, Chapel Hill.

Fabricant, N. and Postero, N. (2015) 'Sacrificing Indigenous Bodies and Lands: The Political–Economic History of Lowland Bolivia in Light of the Recent TIPNIS Debate', *Journal of Latin American and Caribbean Anthropology*, vol 20, no 3, pp452–474.

Farthing, L. (2019) 'An Opportunity Squandered? Elites, Social Movements, and the Government of Evo Morales', *Latin American Perspectives*, Issue 224, vol 46, no 1, pp212–229.

Farthing, L. (2020) 'In Bolivia, the Right Returns with a Vengeance', *NACLA — Report on the Americas*, vol 54, no 3, pp5–12.

Fox, E. ed. (1988) *Media and Politics in Latin America. The Struggle for Democracy.* Sage Publications, London.

Galindo, M. (2020) 'Barricada a Robert Brockman: autor del libro "21 dias de la Resistencia: la caída de Evo Morales"', *Radio Deseo*, 15 October. https://www.youtube.com/watch?v=a-nglKVG2E4

Garcés, F. et al. (2010) *El Pacto de Unidad y el Proceso de construcción de una Propusta de Consittución Política del Estado.* Preview Gráfica, La Paz.

Glenn, J.K. (2003) 'Parties Out of Movements: Party Emergence in Postcommunist Eastern Europe' in Goldstone, J.A. (ed) *States, Parties and Social Movements.* Cambridge University Press, Cambridge.

Goldstone, J.A. (ed) (2013) *States, Parties and Social Movements.* Cambridge University Press, Cambridge.

Goodale, M. (2020) *A Revolution in Fragments. Transversing Scales of Justice, Ideology and Practice in Bolivia'.* Duke University Press, Durham and London.

Gustafson, B. (2009) 'Bolivia 9/11: Bodies and Power on a Feudal Frontier', *Caterwaul Quarterly*, Spring-Summer.

Hollender, R. (2016) 'Capitalizing on Public Discourse in Bolivia – Evo Morales and Twenty-first Century Capitalism'. *Consilience*, Vol 15, pp50–76.

Human Rights Watch (2020) 'Justice as a Weapon. Political Persecution in Bolivia', 11 September. https://www.hrw.org/report/2020/09/11/justice-weapon/political-persecution-bolivia

Infobae (2019) 'El momento en que el líder opositor Fernando Camacho dejó en la Casa de Gobierno la carta de renuncia para que Evo Morales la firme', 10 November. https://www.infobae.com/america/america-latina/2019/11/10/el-momento-en-que-el-lider-opositor-fernando-camacho-dejo-en-la-casa-de-gobierno-la-carta-de-renuncia-para-evo-morales-la-firme/

Inter-American Commission for Human Rights (2020) *Informe Anual de la Comisión Interamericana de Derechos Humanos 2019. Volumen II.* 24 February. http://www.oas.org/es/cidh/expresion/informes/ESPIA2019.pdf

International Human Rights Clinic (2020) *"The Shot Us Like Animals". Black November & Bolivia's Interim Government.* http://hrp.law.harvard.edu/wp-content/uploads/2020/07/Black-November-English-Final_Accessible.pdf

Kenis, P. and Schneider, V. (1991) 'Policy Networks and Policy Analysis: Scrutinizing a New Analytical Toolbox' in Marin, B. and Mayntz, R. (eds) *Policy Networks. Empirical Evidence and Theoretical Considerations*. Campus/Westview, Frankfurt a.M./Boulder.

Kitschelt, H. (2006) 'Party Movements' in Katz, R.S. y Crotty, W. (eds) *Handbook of Party Politics*. Sage Publications Ltd., London.

Kitzberger, P. (2010) 'The Media Activism of Latin America's Leftist Governments: Does Ideology Matter?' GIGA Research Unit, Institute of Latin American Studies, No. 151.

Kitzberger, P. (2012) 'The Media Politics of Latin America's Leftist Governments', *Journal of Politics in Latin America*, vol 3, pp123–139.

Knaack, P. (2020) 'Bolivia: Pulling in Two Directions – The Developmental State and Basel Standards' in E. Jones (ed) *The Political Economy of Bank Regulation in Developing Countries: Risk and Reputation*. Oxford University Press, Oxford.

Laing, A. (2015) 'Resource Sovereignties in Bolivia: Re-Conceptualising the Relationship between Indigenous Identities and the Environment during the TIPNIS Conflict', *Bulletin of Latin American Research*, vol 34, no 2, pp149–166.

Lucero, J.A. (2008) *Struggles of Voice: The Politics of Indigenous Representation in the Andes*. University of Pittsburgh Press, Pittsburgh.

Lupien, P. (2013) 'The Media in Venezuela and Bolivia: Attacking the "Bad Left" form Below', *Latin American Perspectives*, Vol 40, pp226–246.

Mainwaring, S. y Scully, T.R. (1995) *Building Democratic Institutions: Party Systems in Latin America*. Stanford University Press, Stanford.

Mayorga, R.A. (2004) 'La crisis del Sistema de partidos políticos en Bolivia: causas y consecuencias', *Cuadernos del CENDES*, vol 21, no 57, pp83–114.

Mckay, B. et al. (2014) 'The "State" of Food Sovereignty in Latin America: Political Project and Alternative Pathways in Venezuela, Ecuador, and Bolivia', *Journal of Peasant Studies*, vol 41, no 6, pp1175–1200.

Mckay, B. (2020) *The Political Economy of Agrarian Extractivism. Lessons from Bolivia*. Practica Action Publishing Ltd., Rugby.

McNeish, A. (2013) 'Extraction, Protest and Indigeneity in Bolivia: The TIPNIS Effect', *Latin American and Caribbean Ethnic Studies*, vol 8, no 2, pp221–242.

Miranda, B. (2020) 'Coronavirus en Bolivia: un escándalo por la compra de respiradores provoca la destitución del ministro de Salud'. *BBC*, 20 May. https://www.bbc.com/mundo/noticias-52747870

Molina, F. (2020) '¿Por qué volvió a ganar el MAS? Lecturas de las elecciones bolivianas'. *Nueva Sociedad*, October. https://nuso.org/articulo/Bolivia-Luis-Arce-Evo-Morales/

Moseley, M.W. (2018) *Protest State: The Rise of Everyday Contention in Latin America'*. Oxford University Press, New York.

ONADEM (2011) *Medios a la Vista 2. Análisis sobre el Derecho a la Información y la Comunicación y el Periodismo en Bolivia 2009–2011*. Fundación Unir Bolivia, Observatorio Nacional de Medios ONADEM, La Paz.

Opinión (2020) 'En nueve meses de gestión, la presidenta Áñez cambió a 13 ministros', 5 August. https://www.opinion.com.bo/articulo/pais/meses-gestion-presenta-anez-cambio-13-ministros/20200804231231781003.html

Página Siete (2019) 'Según la encuesta, 68% cree que habrá fraude electoral', 29 September. https://www.paginasiete.bo/nacional/2019/9/29/segun-la-encuesta-68-cree-que-habra-fraude-electoral-232481.html

Página Siete (2020) 'Dos "masacres" y corrupción empañanan la gestión de Añez'. 6 November. https://www.paginasiete.bo/nacional/2020/11/6/dos-masacres-corrupcion-empanan-la-gestion-de-anez-273987.html

Pando, A. (2020) 'Camacho, el hotel Casa Grande y las ambiciones de poder', *Cabildeo Digital,* 11 October. http://www.cabildeodigital.com/2020/10/camacho-el-hotel-casa-grande-y-las.html

Peñaranda, R. (2020) 'Razones de la victoria del MAS'. *Brújula Digital*, 24 October. https://brujuladigital.net/opinion/razones-de-la-victoria-del-mas

Perreault, T. and Green, B. (2013) 'Reworking the Spaces of Indigeneity: The Bolivian Ayllu and Lowland Autonomy Movements Compared', *Environment and Planning D: Society and Space*, Vol 31, pp43–60.

Postero, N. (2017) *The Indigenous State: Race, Politics and Performance in Plurinational Bolivia.* University of California Press, Oakland.

Regalsky, P. (2010) 'Political Processes and the Reconfiguration of the State in Bolivia'. *Latin American Perspectives*, vol 37, no 3, pp35–50.

Rivera Cusicanqui, S. (2015) 'Strategic Ethnicity, Nation, and (Neo)Colonialism in Latin America', *Alternautas*, vol 2, no 2, pp10–20.

Roberts, K.M. (1998) *Deepening Democracy? The Modern Left and Social Movements in Chile and Peru.* Stanford University Press, Stanford.

Salman, T. (2011) 'Entre protestar y gobernar. Movimientos sociales en Bolivia en tiempos del MAS', *Tinkazos*, Vol 29, pp21–43.

Schönwalder, G. (1997) 'New Democratic Spaces at the Grassroots? Popular Participation in Latin American Local Governments', *Development and Change*, vol 28, no 4, pp753–770.

Solón, P. (2020) '¿Una Nueva Crisis? Reflecting Upon MAS' Legacy and the Future of Bolivia'. *NACLA* panel discussion, 8 October.

Stefanoni, P. (2020) 'A New MAS Era in Bolivia'. *NACLA*, 21 October. https://nacla.org/news/2020/10/24/new-mas-era-bolivia

Steyn, I. (2012) 'The State and Social Movements: Autonomy and Its Pitfalls', *Politikon: South African Journal of Political Studies*, vol 39, no 3, pp331–351.

Tilly, C. (2007) *Democracy.* Cambridge University Press, New York.

UN Office of the High Commissioner for Human Rights (2020) *The Human Rights Situation in the Aftermath of the 20 October 2019 General Elections in Bolivia.* https://www.ohchr.org/Documents/Countries/BO/OACNUDH-Informe-Bolivia-EN.pdf

Valdivia, S. (2019) *Political Networks and Social Movements. Bolivian State-Society Relations under Evo Morales, 2006–2016.* Berghahn, New York.

Van Cott, D.L. (2000) 'Party System Development and Indigenous Populations in Latin America: The Bolivian Case', *Party Politics*, vol 6, no 2, pp155–174.

Van Cott, D.L. (2005) *From Movements to Parties in Latin America: The Evolution of Ethnic Politics.* Cambridge University Press, Cambridge.

Van Cott, D.L. (2008) *Radical Democracy in the Andes.* Cambridge University Press, Cambridge.

Wolf, J. (2020). 'The Turbulent End of an Era in Bolivia: Contested Elections, the Ouster of Evo Morales, and the Beginning of a Transition towards an Uncertain Future', *Revista de Ciencia Política*, vol 40, no 2, pp163–186.

Zuazo, M. (2010) '¿Los movimientos sociales en el poder? El gobierno del MAS en Bolivia', *Nueva Sociedad*, Vol 227, pp120–135.

3 Crisis time, class formation and the end of Evo Morales

Angus McNelly

Introduction

The months of October–November 2019 transformed the political context in Bolivia and marked a confusing end to the government of Evo Morales—I say this as, a year on, it is still not entirely clear what happened. The 20 October elections were overshadowed by accusations of fraud and followed by two weeks punctuated by violence. After 14 years in power, Morales was forced from office at the suggestion of the military in the wake of police mutiny across the country. Right-wing senator Jeanine Áñez formed an interim government and entered the presidential palace, bible in hand, declaring the return of the republic. Indigenous signs and symbols were ripped down and burnt, provoking a violent reaction in the Aymara city of El Alto, where groups of indignant residents marched through the streets calling for an immediate civil war. Retribution from the new regime was swift, with dozens killed by the military in the El Alto neighbourhood of Senkata and in the coca-growing town of Sacaba, Cochabamba. The political scenario polarised, with both sides digging themselves into their respective positions—*electoral fraud* or *coup d'état*—and refusing to budge.

In light of this, dissecting this conjuncture is not an easy task and is fraught with not only the normal difficulties one encounters when studying Bolivia but the added challenge of intense politicisation, even within academic circles. In order to overcome these significant obstacles, I propose returning to Bolivian political theorist René Zavaleta Mercado and his late work diagnosing the crisis of the National Revolutionary State (1952–early 1980s). Here Zavaleta situates his theoretical concepts in historical context and traces the historic processes of state formation, nation-building, the emergence of historic blocs and political economy across multiple temporalities—namely the *longue durée* and the medium-term. For Zavaleta, a crisis is not simply destructive and problematic but

> is an anomalous instance in the life of a society, that is to say, a time when things do not present themselves as they are in everyday life, but, for a change, a time when things appear as they truly are. (Zavaleta 2008: 19)

Following Zavaleta's lead, I contend the October–November crisis offers a lens through which to discern the formation of both the social forces that began to emerge towards the end of Morales' premiership and the conflicting narratives that predominated during this period.

The chapter is structured into four sections. I start by laying the theoretical foundations of the argument, drawing on the work of Zavaleta. Next, I briefly sketch out the different social forces present in this moment. I then, in section three, evaluate the political economy contours of Morales' time in power and the contradictory outcomes that they produced, explaining the social composition of each group. Finally, I look at two competing projects of nation-building—plurinationalism and regional autonomy—to explore the attraction of different political projects and the genesis of the two competing discourses (fraud and coup d'état) on the crisis.

Theory, history and temporalities: thinking with René Zavaleta

René Zavaleta (1937–1984) is considered by many to be Bolivia's greatest thinker (see Thomson 2019; Webber 2011a). It's hard to argue with this contention, as Zavaleta's approach traverses old divides—structure/agency, theory/history, the particular/the universal—to build a conceptual framework that is simultaneously spatially and temporally sensitive to specific historical conjunctures and able to speak to other historical and geographical contexts (see Freeland 2019: 276; Lagos Rojas 2018). Although at times labyrinthine and open (see Dunkerley 2013), the body of Zavaleta's work provides powerful conceptual tools to tie together the multiple dynamics leading to, and at play during, the crisis during October–November 2019 in Bolivia.

Zavaleta's method contains 'both specific historical-political and general conceptual angles' (Thomson 2019: 84), and bridges the gap, as he himself says (Zavaleta 2008: 80), between the Marx (1982[1867]) of *Capital* and the Marx (1978[1851]) of *The Eighteenth Brumaire of Louis Bonaparte*. Drawing on Fernand Braudel (2009), one of Zavaleta's great interpreters, Luis Tapia (2019: 132), proposes that rather than thinking about this divide in Zavaleta's work as one between history and theory, it is more productive to consider the different layers encountered in Zavaleta as an analysis of 'how *longue durée* conditions cut across medium-term structures'. On the one hand, Tapia (2019: 132) contends that over the *longue durée*, Zavaleta's central concern is the 'operation of the law of value, that is, the processes of generalisation of the abstraction of labour, or of the expansion of the capitalist mode of production on a global scale'. The *longue durée* conditions determine 'the epistemic constraints of structural position within a global order [that] are taken for granted' in Zavaleta's work (Freeland 2016: 278). Over this temporality, on the most abstract level Zavaleta evaluates modes of production, that is to say, the aggregate social relations of production that form the economic structure of a society and 'the social, political and intellectual life process in general' that emanate from such arrangements of social relations (see Marx 1977).

On a more concrete level (yet still over the *longue durée*), Zavaleta turns his attention to civilisation and societal forms. Civilisational forms, explains Tapia (2016a: 19–24), are determined by historical time and the transformation of nature (Thomson 2019: 90), whilst societal forms are 'determined by the mode of articulation between the mode of production, type of societal structures, forms of government and types of organisations and cultures' (Tapia 2016a: 21). Whilst societal and civilisation forms initially appear as abstract formulations, they capture the persistence of indigenous social and political practices and relations within Bolivia today, even as all indigenous communities are subsumed under the logic of capitalism. However, even though the market has penetrated indigenous communities and forms the economic basis for their reproduction, capitalist relations 'do not prevail thoroughly and effectively' and other social relations based on alternative logics—such as the reciprocal logic of *ayni* and *mink'a*[1]—continue to play an important part in shaping Bolivian society (Thomson 2019: 89). Societal and civilisational forms help capture the longer trajectories of coloniality at play in Latin America and position indigenous communities (as well as movements) as central political actors.

On the other hand, 'structures of medium-term duration … correspond to national histories' and in particular the changing interactions between nation, state and civil society (Tapia 2019: 131). This is one of the exciting elements of Zavaleta: despite recognising Latin America's dependent position within the global market and system of nation states, he stresses the salience of 'political self-determination' (Zavaleta 2008: 12) and 'the possibility of rupture and of a reorganization of [dependent] conditions, which are necessarily both limiting and enabling' (Freeland 2016: 278). Zavaleta is particularly interested in what, in his esoteric vocabulary, he labels *primordial forms* and *constitutive moments*. The primordial form captures the local historical determinants within each, particular social formation, whilst concurrently accounting for the structures of regional and global power that shape the terrain over which these local factors play out (Tapia 2002: 282–285; Zavaleta 1982). As such, it addresses the 'relation between state and civil society in the history of each country ... and allows us to think [through] the articulation of the different dimensions of social life in particular territories and at particular times' (Tapia 2019: 131).

The constitutive movement addresses the foundational moments of social change (nationalising moments), when there is a willingness or receptiveness to new ideas and ideologies across society (Zavaleta 2008: 37). Evaluating constitutive moments is so fertile precisely because it entails the examination of the interplay between the processes constructing social blocs with a 'national reach' (Zavaleta 2008: 11) and a society's readiness to embrace change—something that requires a shared history [*aconteciminetos communes*] and a shared psychology to work in tandem to produce a new society (Zavaleta 2008: 37). Zavaleta calls this willingness *disponibilidad*, which encompasses 'a society's readiness (a cognate would be "disposition") to receive or respond to the interpellation of a new hegemonic project,[2] to fundamentally alter its conception of the world and of itself' (Freeland 2016: 272).

There are three elements of constitutive moments: (1) primitive accumulation; (2) formal subsumption; and (3) real subsumption. Zavaleta (2013a: 620) re-reads Marx to conceptualise each of these moments as *political* transformations. Primitive accumulation is the creation of legally equal individuals through their detachment from the land. Formal subsumption is the moment when 'interpellation can take place, that is, the suppression of the hollowing-out [moment] from a determinate viewpoint or character' thanks to the subordination of labour to capital. Finally, real subsumption is 'the application of the conscious gnosis as well as of the masses' power—and other high-quality powers—to the previous factors: capital as effective command and free men [sic] in a mass-status'. For Zavaleta (2008: 36), the *sine qua non* of capitalism is the juridically free person, that is to say, a (new) political subject. Primitive accumulation, formal and real subsumption, in Zavaleta's framework, do not just capture the economic transformation of productive relations by capital but also the new political subjectivities and collectivities—particularly the nation—which emerge through these changes.

Sociedades Abigarradas and crisis as method

Returning to the conditions of constitutive moments, *disponibilidad* is the pre-condition that permits the totalisation of capital under the stewardship of the capitalist state. *Disponibilidad*, or the disposition of a society to a new set of political ideas, is the foundation of a hegemonic political project and, more specifically, state hegemony (Zavaleta 2008: 78). In the case of societies marked by multiple overlapping modes of production (and consequently a multiplicity of societal and civilisational forms), the hegemony of the state requires the flattening of multiple temporalities into what Zavaleta labels *state time* (Lagos Rojas 2018: 137).

Zavaleta introduces the concept of *sociedades abigarradas* to capture situations where the multiple temporalities of manifold modes of production, and civilisation and societal formations are not contained within the homogenous time of the state; that is to say, contexts where the state fails to become hegemonic (see Lagos Rojas 2018: 140). *Abigarrada* or *abigarramiento* roughly translate as motley or heterogeneous and 'connote disjointedness, incongruousness, beyond mere difference' (Freeland 2016: 272). Zavaleta's characterisation of Bolivia as a *sociedad abigarrada* captures the concrete historical articulation of multiple modes of production—the organisation of productive forces by different forms and grades of the development of productive relations—and how these articulations (re-) produce multiple civilisational and societal forms. In other words, *abigarramiento* provides a tool with which to study the interplay between the *longue durée* conditions and medium-term structures in concrete historical moments.

However, there is an epistemological paradox that comes with framing societies such as Bolivia as *abigarrada*: it implies that they are unknowable and unrepresentable societies precisely *because of* their *abigarramiento*. Zavaleta insists on what he considers to be an imperfect methodology to study such contexts, whereby theoretical categories are always historically qualified and contextualised (Freeland 2019: 276). Indeed, Zavaleta (2008: 9) starts his unfinished Magnum Opus *Lo nacional-popular en Bolivia* on a rueful note, stating that this is the only form of social science possible in contexts of *abigarramiento* like Bolivia. However, he does offer a way out of his theoretical cul-de-sac through *crisis as method* (see Zavaleta 2013b). For Zavaleta, crisis is the critical manifestation of the multiple social forces and their multiple associated civilisational times, which share as a common time, that of politics. In other words, in the absence of a hegemonic state and its *state time*, crisis provides synchronism through a shared political moment, something that in turn unveils the complex and enigmatic social reality in places like Bolivia. After all, crisis is not preparation for what is to come but an *accumulation of what has already come to pass*, and as such, 'not only reveals what is national in Bolivia, but that which is itself a nationalising event' (Zavaleta 2013b: 216).

The goal of this section has been to underscore the importance—simultaneously political and epistemological—of the crisis of October–November, both as the accumulation of intertwined historical processes and as a lens through which we can examine and evaluate the *sociedad abigarrada* of Bolivia. The crisis offers a historical conjuncture in which to study the dynamics and social effects rippling out from processes of state formation, nation-building, class formation and capitalist accumulation, as well as the ideological and discursive terrain over which the crisis unfurled. Whilst these are expansive tasks that extend well beyond the scope of this chapter, I will tentatively offer a preliminary sketch of the interplay between these elements in the period leading to the October–November crisis.

Socio-economic composition of crisis

Before turning to the pathways that led to the crisis, it is necessary to sketch the socio-economic composition of the crisis, to dissect the historic blocs present at this moment. At the social base of the MAS are the peasant organisations of the Andean highlands [*altiplano*] and the semi-tropical valleys of Cochabamba, the Unified Syndicalist Confederation of Peasant Workers of Bolivia (CSUTCB) and the Six Federations of the Tropics of Cochabamba, respectively, as well as the Syndicalist Confederation of Intercultural Communities of Bolivia (CSCIB, formerly Trade-Union Confederation of Colonizers, CSCB). These organisations, which represent peasants and rural proletarian labourers, have an organic relationship with the MAS and as such all turned out to vote for and defend it on the streets (McNelly 2020c).[3]

This hard core of social support was complemented by sectors that had benefitted from the politics of the MAS. These included the swathes of the informalised petty commodity producers and hidden wage labourers found in the popular economy; sections of the cooperative and state-employed miners; and sections of the lower middle classes and professional classes who felt Morales had both reduced the stigma they confront in their day-to-day lives and offered them inclusion and representation within the liberal parliamentary system of democracy.[4]

However, despite this continued support, by 2019 the MAS had burned its bridges with many former social organisation allies during its time in power. During its first term (2006–2009), the central demands of the social movements (2000–2005) were incorporated into the political project of the MAS through technocratic means. So, in March 2006, the government put the wheels in motion for a Constituent Assembly to rewrite the constitution, whilst in May 2006 it proclaimed the nationalisation of gas. Organisation leaders were offered positions in Morales' cabinet and swathes more joined the ranks of the swelling state bureaucracy. Many saw the MAS and Evo Morales as *their* government and so were more than happy to align as the social base of the MAS (I will touch on this further below). Nevertheless, this had contradictory consequences as social organisations lost the ability to respond to their bases as they became more and more driven by top-down directives.[5] By late-2019, social organisations had become empty shells with little to no internal democracy or self-critique, morbid entities whose moribund state was plain for all to see when the MAS called for mass protests in defence of Morales during the run-up to his exit on 10 November and nobody answered.[6]

The opposition to the MAS was also comprised of multiple different—and contradictory—currents. First, there was a group concerned with the abstract notion of *democracy*—understood in its narrowest, liberal representative form—comprised of the urban middle-classes and university students largely under the age of 25 (Galindo 2020: 23). These 'intermediary classes' (see Braga 2019) were probably the largest oppositional group and was found in all nine departmental capitals. The second group were indigenous groups that did not share the productivist/developmentalist agenda of the MAS government and/or were in the pathway of extractivism or large-scale infrastructure projects. The lowland indigenous groups, particularly those in the Isiboro Sécure National Park and Indigenous Territory (TIPNIS), groups in the Chaco regions affected by hydrocarbon extraction, the groups in the Madidi national park opposing the mega dams Bala and Chapete and the *ayllus* of North Potosí were the most visible elements of this opposition. The prominent organisation matrices of this second oppositional strand were the highland indigenous organisation, Consejo Nacional de Ayllus y Markas del Qullasuyu (CONAMAQ), and the lowland organisation, Confederación de Pueblos Indígenas de Bolivia (CIDOB), both of whom had been in open conflict with the MAS since 2011 (Hylton and Webber 2019).

Finally, there was the regional opposition concerned with the distribution of power and resources within the country. The indigenous opposition to Morales in the city of Potosí can be categorised as part of this group, as can the civic committees of Beni, Pando, Santa Cruz and Tarija (the Media Luna departments). There are similarities between this latter group and the autonomy movement of 2003–2008, which formed the major opposition to Morales during his first term. However, there are some important differences, with emergence of a hitherto little-known figure, Luis Fernando Camacho, from the backwaters of regional, right-wing politics in Santa Cruz to national politics. Along with Korean-Bolivian presidential candidate Chi Hyun Chung, Camacho spoke of 'bringing the bible to Bolivian congress' and marked the first serious articulation of the evangelical Right (so present elsewhere in Latin America) in Bolivian national politics. He was one of the more prominent figures calling for military intervention, and helped created the conditions that allowed more extreme oppositional groups to burn down the houses of several prominent MAS allies and ministers during the night of 9 November (McNelly 2019).

There was, in the midst of this crisis, situated in-between MAS and oppositional factions, an important feminist current focused on breaking down the growing polarisation and opposing the racketing up of violence (Gutiérrez 2020: 10; Zibechi 2020: 33–34). Intellectually, this strand drew on the decolonial scholarship of Silvia Rivera (the most well-known of Zavaleta's students) and ex-Comuna member Raquel Gutiérrez to try and breakdown the Manichean logic of the crisis. In other words, this feminist bloc worked precisely to destabilise the shared time of political crisis and to reassert the multitude and multiplicity of Bolivia's *sociedad abigarrada*. The anarcho-feminist collective, Mujeres Creando, organised a women's parliament, which provided a vital space for reflection on the causes of the crisis and the limitations of the political project of Morales. Here I want to take up this feminist blocs' call to examine the dynamics of Morales' tenure as president in order to fully grasp how we arrived at the moment under consideration here.

Capital accumulation and class formation in Bolivia

Arguably, no one has done more than Evo Morales and his government to transform the political economy of Bolivia. Under his tenure, the government captured more natural resource rent than ever before, thanks to the renegotiation of contracts with hydrocarbon producers and the (retrospectively) savvy signing of medium-term, fixed-price export contracts with Argentina and Brazil (Haarstad 2014; Kaup 2010;

Webber 2011a). The MAS government then directed this extra surplus into redistributive policies, including conditional cash transfers and higher formal wages, increasing the consumption of popular sectors and forming what political ecologist Eduardo Gudynas (2012) labels a *compensatory state*. The results on social indicators were positive: according to United Nations Economic Commission for Latin American and the Caribbean (ECLAC 2017) calculations, absolute poverty fell from 38.2% in 2005 to 15.2% in 2017, and the index for income inequality, the Gini coefficient, dropped from 58.5 in 2005 to 44 in 2017. On the surface, at least, the Bolivian economy went from strength to strength during the Morales years.

Rather predictably, if we dig a little deeper, the picture becomes muddied somewhat. The political economy of Bolivia is still shaped by conditions of dependency and its peripheral place in the global market, having been inserted into the global economy initially as a source of silver, later a source of tin and, more recently, as a hydrocarbon-rich country. This means that hydrocarbons comprise around 50% of the value of all exports (despite only accounting for under 15% of GDP) before other mineral and metal material exports are considered (McNelly 2020b). The upshot of Bolivia's position as a primary commodity producer is that it remains dependent on primary commodity extraction for the dynamism of capital accumulation (see Mendes Loureiro 2018), and, due to the relatively undiversified nature of its economy and the volatility of global commodity prices, it is comparatively sensitive to developments elsewhere in the global economy. The end of the commodity super cycle (2002–2011) placed increasing strain on the final two terms of Morales' presidency, and the October 2019 elections took place among the backdrop of falling commodity prices globally (ECLAC 2019a: 24). This affected hydrocarbon and mineral-exporting countries across South America and ate away at regional trade surpluses, as a fall in the value of exports eroded trade balances and contributed to growing balance of payment deficits across the region (ECLAC 2019b: 46).

Despite running a balance of payments surplus until 2014 (McNelly 2020b: 432), by 2019, Bolivia's balance of payments deficit was US$860m, largely because the importation of capital goods (US$1.9bn), vehicles and machinery (US$1.3bn) and consumables (US$1.0bn) continued to outstrip the exportation of hydrocarbons (US$2.8bn) (INE 2020). The sluggish demand for Bolivian exports (ECLAC 2019a: 47)—itself a consequence of slowing global growth (particularly in the motor of the global economy, China) and the shockwaves emanating from the trade war between China and US that began in 2017—have been accompanied by a drop in Foreign Direct Investment (FDI) inflows, highlighted by a reduction of Net Foreign Direct Investment flows from a high of US$1.75bn in 2013 to US$344m in 2018 (ECLAC 2019a: 203). More worrisome still, natural gas production has also been declining since 2014, 'plunging in the last quarter of 2018 by 24% compared to the same period of 2017, a decrease which has not been reversed in the first quarter of 2019' (ECLAC 2019a: 46). This suggests that the reduction of hydrocarbon revenue is not only due to external factors linked to global commodity prices and Bolivia's two biggest export markets (Argentina and Brazil) but also due to technical constraints on domestic production.

These conditions of dependency do not determine, but rather shape and intersect with, the socio-political structures and ephemeral political events in Bolivia. As such, they tell only part of the story of the political-economic trajectory of Bolivia under Morales. Even with an impressive formal minimum wage growth of over 100% in real terms between 2005 and 2015 (ILO 2017: 65), the growth in the share of GDP paid in wages was below the regional average (0.15% increase over the same period), which is hardly spectacular given the very modest share of GDP paid in wages in the first place (ILO 2017: 81). The effect of the rising minimum wage but not the overall wage share was to reduce the difference between the minimum and average wages but not to improve employment prospects for the population, which was a particular gripe of the increasingly well-educated middle-classes and aspiration working-class people.[7] This would have political ramifications in the later years of Morales' presidency, as these groups scrambled around for the few jobs that matched their educational attainment.

The absolute size of the economically active population (EAP) did not change under the Morales years, continuing to hover around 65% of the population (75% of men, 57% of women) over the 15 years he was in power (INE 2020). Given that the size of the EAP as a proportion of the population captures the grade of dependence on wage-labour in a society, this is hardly surprising. Formal subsumption in Bolivia was, by and large, completed by the last massive wave of entry into the labour market during the late-1980s and early 1990s, when the EAP grew by roughly 50% in five years (Arze and Maita Pérez 2000: 37). During this period, the opening up of agriculture markets to the global economy undermined the ability of indigenous and peasant communities to survive, increasing market penetration in rural areas and forcing their increasingly degraded population into the labour market. Erstwhile peasants were joined by the wives and daughters of former state employees and miners tossed out of the home and into the workplace by neoliberal restructuring (sees Gill 1994; Rivera 1996). Such is the degree of generalised dependence on wage-labour for survival after the violence of this moment, that there were not many more people to join the ranks of the EAP by the time Morales assumed office. The large swathes of people who worked in the popular economy were supportive of Morales for much of his tenure, identifying with him as *hermano* (brother) Evo, the country's first indigenous president. They were also generally satisfied with their increasing incomes thanks to the massive expansion of capital circulating through informal circuits, as the growing resource rents captured by the state were recycled through increases in the national minimum wage and conditional cash transfers (see Tassi et al. 2013; Webber 2016). However, popular economy actors were not tied to Morales institutionally (like the coca growers were), and growing affluence, coupled with frustrated middle-class aspirations, undermined some of the support Morales enjoyed from this group during his later years in power.

Whilst formal subsumption appears all but complete in the 21st-century Bolivia, the stubborn persistence of the popular economy suggests that real subsumption remains partial at best in Bolivia. The continuing significance of the popular economy reveals the limited extent to which Bolivian social and economic life has been reorganised to fit the technological and organisational needs of capital. It is in a large part to the high instance of commercial and service activities orientated towards the (relatively) minuscule internal market. This is, undoubtedly, a condition of dependency, as large-scale capital investment continues to be in either extractive processes or large-scale infrastructure projects, both of which require very little labour, and have few forward and backward linkages with the rest of the Bolivian economy (see McNelly 2020b).

There are, nevertheless, other signs that real subsumption is creeping along in Bolivia. One possible indicator of the steadily increasing penetration of capital into all spheres of Bolivian society is the percentage of the population living in urban areas, which has grown from 61.8% of the Bolivian population in 2000 to 69.4% in 2018 (World Bank 2020). Many, if not most, of the people who make up this migrant stream are young people leaving rural communities in search of a better life in Bolivian cities, with the draw of the three central metropolitan areas of the country (La Paz/El Alto, Cochabamba and Santa Cruz) being such that they accounted for over half of Bolivia's population by 2012 (INE 2012).[8] These migration flows have been accompanied by the growing urbanisation of rural areas, as new city residents use surplus acquired under the bright city lights (or, in many cases, in their shadows) to construct new multi-storey brick houses and to wall off previously collectivised territory (Horn 2018). This has transformed societal and civilisational forms, as the social practices of organising and governing (for want of a better word) indigenous communities are disrupted by the exodus of young generations and clashes between commercial and collective use of land. The reliance of land for all food and subsistence goods has been weakened as communities become increasingly penetrated by market logics. These distortions to societal and civilisational forms have altered the composition of indigenous movements and what it means to be indigenous in the process.[9]

The other side of this creeping real subsumption is the encroachment of extractive activities into indigenous territories, either through the expansion of the agricultural frontier to quell the insatiable thirst of mono-crop production, or through the displacement of communities by the construction of megaprojects—be it highways, as was the case with the conflict of the TIPNIS (McNeish 2013), or hydroelectric dams, as is the case with the Bala and Chepete (Véliz 2016). The state's dependence on primary resources reproduces the logic of coloniality: the commodification of nature, the marking of territory holding minerals, metals or hydrocarbons as dispensable and the disregard for the communities and human lives that lie in the way of capital's pathway to these resources (Salazar 2015). That this was a feature of the Bolivian state fostered under the MAS government is clear from reading the accounts of the October–November crisis given by activists and scholars who have been politically engaged in the country for decades (see in particular Paley 2020). One of Morales' principal limitations was that he reproduced the very same colonial logics he ostensibly opposed and the social conflicts that this generated under the MAS government—particularly between the government and numerous indigenous groups—marked the crisis as it unfolded in the tense days of October and November.

Drawing together the different political-economic threads outlined in this section starts to illuminate some of the obscured dynamics behind the crisis. Bolivia remained constrained by its peripheral position in the global economy as a primary commodity producer, and despite attempts to use the surpluses extractive activities generate to transform society, the results were limited. The structure of the labour force remained similar, and informal activities in the popular economy continued to assume centre stage both in the country's quotidian life and in the labour market. Although the minimum wage rose and the average educational level of the workforce increased, the jobs on offer remained the same. The middle classes saw increasing competition for the limited government and professional jobs they considered rightfully theirs and grumbled. The aspirant working classes groused when the growing educational attainment of their children did not lead them out of employment in the popular economy. And all the while, extractive activities continued to encounter indigenous communities, a dynamic which pitted the government of Evo Morales against the people he supposedly represented.

Competing narratives and social blocs

> Mr President, from the bottom of our hearts and with great sadness we ask: Where did you get lost? Why don't you live within the ancestral beliefs that says we should respect the *muyu* (circle): that we should govern only once? Why have you sold off our Pachamama? Why did you have the Chiquitanía burned? Why did you so mistreat our Indigenous brothers in Chaparina and Tariquía?
>
> (Qhara Qhara manifesto, cited in Zibechi 2020: 30)

The sentiment of the Qhara Qhara manifesto is one often repeated by indigenous groups across Bolivia: a sense that Evo Morales was an indigenous president (or at least their representative) who had a chance to break with the previous colonial and neoliberal forms of government, and somewhere along the way, he got lost. In fact, during fieldwork between January 2016 and May 2017, very few social organisation leaders or activists I spoke to were critical of Morales himself, despite their despair at (and, at times, loathing of) his government. The reasons for this are complex, but here I want to suggest that following the five-year cycle of social movements against neoliberalism at the start of the millennium, a moment of political opportunity opened, when there was a general receptiveness to new political ideas and to change amongst the general population. For many Bolivians, brother Evo was finally a representative in power who was one of them. The 60-plus per cent of Bolivians who turned out to vote for Morales in the 2009 and 2014 presidential elections believed in the political ideas underpinning his government: plurinationalism, *vivir bien* and 'process of change'. As the latter suggests, people wanted change, and it was the ripples of these affective sentiments towards Evo Morales that, in part, made him so popular for so many years. Here I am going to trace one of these ideals—plurinationalism—from its conception by highland indigenous movements to government policy, and the emergence of its negation found in the regional autonomy movement, to underscore the general *disponibilidad* of the Bolivian population and highlight some of the limitations of plurinationalism as a nationalising moment. I have chosen plurinationalism as it was a concept that was central to the indigenous movements that pushed Morales to power and one of their principal demands in the Constituent Assembly (2006–2007) during the first term of the MAS. It has also become one of the more controversial changes the MAS attempted to implement, making it a good lens through which to examine the generalised *disponibilidad* of this moment.

Plurinationalism emerged from the (mainly Aymara) highland indigenous movements in a situation of continuing internal colonialism. For anthropologist Salvador Schavelzon (2015: 72–78), plurinationalism was a political articulation of the Aymara peasant experience during the 1970s and 1980s, initially crystallising within the Katarismo movement and struggles against the dictatorship of Hugo Banzer.[10] This was furthered by the formation of the Trade-Union Confederation of Bolivian Peasant Workers (CSUTCB) in 1979, which proposed 'an alternative, plurinational model of state, recognising cultural and ethnic diversity and indigenous autonomies' (Powęska 2013: 118). Plurinationalism gained increasing traction following the implementation of neoliberal multiculturalism by President Gonzalo Sánchez de Lozada in the mid-1990s. It offered an alternative to political and economic assimilation into the neoliberal project under the guise of cultural difference and 'the possibility of being simultaneously a member of the Bolivian nation and of a nation at the sub-state level, such as the Aymara, Chiriguana or Moxeña nation' (Nuñez del Prado 2009: 55). Plurinationalism was then radicalised by former Túpaj Katari Guerrilla Army (EGTK) member Felipe Quispe during his leadership of the CSUTCB in the late-1990s, becoming a means for rural Aymara communities and *ayllus* to pursue 'a politics of indigenous uprising and revolt against the republic of whites and Europeans' (Schavelzon 2015: 77).

However, it was not until the formation of the indigenous social movement coalition, the Unity Pact,[11] in 2004 and the election of Morales as President in late-2005 that plurinationalism assumed centre stage. One of the central demands to be articulated through the cycle of social movement struggle was the call for a Constituent Assembly, which the Unity Pact envisioned as being underpinned by plurinationalism, whereby 'the indigenous, originary and peasant nations and peoples of Bolivia would have direct representation in all government levels and powers as collective subjects, in accordance with their customary practices' (Pacto de Unidad 2006: 5). The MAS government took this concept on board, using it as a cornerstone in its project to build an 'indigenous state' (Postero 2017). Through the figure of Morales himself, the MAS were able to present itself as the representative of indigenous groups in Bolivia whilst also fostering national support beyond indigenous groups. However, as the MAS stretched the notion of plurinationalism over its broad support base, it lost some of its specificity, becoming so loose that was effectively transformed into 'a new national identity close to "Bolivianness" itself' (Schavelzon 2015: 79). Indeed, plurinationalism became so intertwined with the Bolivian national identity that it was incorporated into the official name of the country. I contend that Rafael Bautista's (2011: 94) observation about its sister concept, *vivir bien* (living well), can be extended to plurinationalism: it 'does not capture a theoretical but, in its ultimate instance, a political endeavour … what it addresses is the constitution of the subject itself within a political project'. In other words, a brief examination of plurinationalism shows not only the importance of the rise of the peasant moment in the latter stages of the 20th century in shaping Bolivian politics but, more importantly for my argument here, the general *disponibilidad* across the nation to accept a new political reference point and the formation of a new national political identity.

This was not, as I mentioned above, uncontested. Plurinationalism did not just take root in the indigenous movements of the western highland and Cochabamba valleys, later being taken on by the MAS government. It took hold within the circles of the lowland elite, who saw plurinationalism as an existential threat to the economic and political privileges that their class and race had bestowed upon them thanks to the continuing influence of colonial matrices of political power in constructing social hierarchies (Plata 2008: 102). At the turn of the century, the proclamations of 'two Bolivias' by Felipe Quispe sparked a bellicose reaction from this group, who quickly articulated into a political movement around regional autonomy. The result was the emergence of the Media Luna regional bloc and two distinct political projects:

> one that want[ed] to constitute Bolivia through the presence of the indigenous majority, with the constitution of a plurinational state; and the other of the *cruceña* elite, which postulate[d] autonomous departments and, within their radical sectors, the ethnic reinvention of the 'Nación Camba' [Camba Nation].
>
> (Plata 2008: 102)[12]

At the heart of this movement was an alternative vision of the nation, complete with its own distinct ethnic composition and foundational myth.[13] As such, the autonomy movement, and particularly one of its central currents, the Nación Camba, set up their opposition to the MAS government explicitly on the terrain of nationalising projects, with parts of the autonomy movement apparently willing to amputate gangrenous limbs from its body in order to scrape together the foundational materials of its project. In its pursuit of this end, the autonomy movement became increasingly belligerent, threatening to split the country in two. The political tensions reached their zenith in mid-2008, when the departmental governors, supported by their Civic Committees and, at times, protofascist thugs, attempted to mount a coup d'état against Morales with the backing of the US government (Soruco 2011; Webber 2011a; Wikileaks 2015).

In a sense, then, the left-indigenous bloc pushing for plurinationalism and the lowland Media Luna autonomy movement can be considered co-constituted—both driven by ideas, albeit conflicting, of social transformation. Whilst the autonomy movement was nominally defeated in the wake of the violence of the Porvenir massacre in September 2008, the political sentiments and disgruntlement of the lowland elites did not disappear. Although the lowland agricultural bourgeoisie benefitted nicely from the politics of agrarian change pursued by Morales' government (see Castañón 2017; McKay 2018; Wolff 2016), they were not Morales' natural allies, and their alliance with Morales consummated at the 2010 International Fair of Santa Cruz (ExpoCruz) was (as history now shows) little more than a marriage of convenience. When the bonanza of the commodities boom ended and there was not enough of the pie to go around, this group became increasingly agitated and had turned on Morales by the beginning of 2016.

This is the shortcoming of a programme of political reforms without a revolutionary rupture (and the defeat of the old): that a new set of ideas can displace the moral driver of politics and themselves become the new, 'revolutionary' idea (Zavaleta 2008: 42). As much happened in February 2016, when Morales ill-advisedly decided to organise a referendum on the removal of constitutional presidential term limits. Given that Morales had won the national elections two years prior with 61% of the vote, this was not a massive gamble, although it would turn out to be a significant political misjudgement. Disparate oppositional groups were able to unite under the banner of democracy, recycling the initial critiques of the MAS during the Constituent Assembly levied against Morales by his opponents. The plebiscite was framed as the destruction of Bolivian democracy, a threat to the health of the political system regardless of the outcome. In the context of the lack of formal employment opportunities and the increasingly evident accumulation of sectors of the emergent popular bourgeoisie in the economy, the disgruntled urban middle classes gradually drew a connection between plurinationalism and the erasure of democracy, as it increasingly collapsed, together with the MAS, into the figure of Morales. Likewise, the contradictions thrown up by the extractive development model of the MAS undermined the presentation of Morales, and by extension plurinationalism, as the representative of indigenous peoples, helping build cross-class, cross-regional alliances across the different sectors of the opposition to the MAS.

In the days running up to the vote, Morales' opponents were speculating fraud and questioning the legitimacy of the vote right up until the results were announced: a narrow defeat for Morales. A decisive factor in the vote was a series of misinformation campaigns. Doctored images of voting results suggesting that the Supreme Electoral Tribunal (TSE) had engaged in fraud appeared on social media (Gustafson 2016). Although they were later to be shown to be false and, given the referendum result, were ultimately not politically significant, they did set a precedent and sow the seeds of doubt about the TSE. There was also plenty of speculation around the existence (or not) of a child Morales supposedly had with former girlfriend Gabriela Zapata (McNelly 2016), leading the MAS to label the referendum *el día de la mentira* (the day of the lie).

It is in these two lineages that the two competing narratives around the October–November crisis lie: in the opposition who saw (and had always seen) Morales as a threat to Bolivian democracy (understood by some reactionary factions as the old Republic); and in the (real) threat of foreign and/or military-induced regime change. These two narratives—painted by many as dichotomous—emerge from the accumulated political processes of the Morales years. Further doubts were cast when, contravening the outcomes of the 2016 referendum, the TSE accepted Morales' candidacy for the 2019 elections on the basis of his human rights to democracy, and the months leading to the 2019 elections were replete with stories of impending fraud (Chávez V. 2019; Lizárraga 2019). The MAS attempted to counter these accusations by underscoring the possibility of a *coup d'état* (ANF 2019). This is, in part, why both narratives surfaced long before the vote on 20 October took place, and why both sides were quick to decry 'fraud' or 'coup' without a shred of evidence. Viewing the crisis of October–November in this light brings the genealogy of these competing discourses to the fore and helps us understand the political polarisation of this moment.

Conclusion

It is difficult not to hear resonance with the arguments presented by Zavaleta in *Lo nacional-popular en Bolivia* in the crisis of late-2019. I have drawn on Zavaleta's method of examining how *longue durée* conditions intersect with medium-term structures in order to place the contentious events of October–November 2019 in context. This was a crisis marked by *both* continuity *and* change: it represented the culmination of political, economic and social processes started under the Morales government, and yet it also contained a rupture with the old, as Morales and his party were disposed from power. I sketched out the political-economic dimensions of the past 20 years in Bolivia, exploring how the development model pursued by the MAS within the structural constraints of dependency undermined its support amongst the urban middle-classes and upwardly mobile working classes and put Morales' government on a collision course with indigenous communities in the pathway of infrastructure projects and extractive activities. I also examined the limitations of plurinationalism as a nationalising project and how it emerged alongside a regional autonomy movement that acted as its political negation. I explained how discourses and practices of these two political poles developed over the 15 years of Morales' presidency and ossified into the cartography of *fraud* and *coup d'état* upon which the struggles over framing the crisis of late-2019 took place.

On a more theoretical plane, one of the major contributions of the chapter has been to renew Zavaleta's method of using crisis as a window through which to study Bolivian society. The theoretical development of Zavaleta's method here is only partial—there is plenty more to be done in order to realise the potential of this approach—but it does point to the power of using a historical conjuncture when the historical sediments of the past have been kicked up and placed in relation to one another through the shared time of politics. This offers a powerful lens through which to examine political developments within postcolonial contexts and draw connections between seemingly disparate processes: in this case, between more structural processes of formal subsumption, real subsumption, class formation and the ephemeral political processes constructing class alliances (historic blocs) and political discourses. I would tentatively add here that crisis as a method offers a way to bridge the study of processes of capitalist development and postcoloniality and to reconcile the vexed relationship between Marxism and postcolonial theory (see Rao 2017; Rutazibwa and Shilliam 2018).

Taking a step back from this analysis, I want to suggest some more general lessons to glean from the analysis presented here. On a theoretical note, it is clear that the work of René Zavaleta still has much to give to contemporary social science well beyond the Bolivian context. By stressing the historical specificity of universal processes and the importance of being sensitive to *both* spatially and temporally particularities *and* generalised capitalist dynamics, Zavaleta encourages the *breaking open* of theory developed in other contexts (rather than its mechanical application) and invites scholarship that, as stated earlier, learns *from* rather than *about* specific historical moments. His methodology for thinking at the periphery of capitalism is immensely rich, and I can only hope that the renewed interest in his work, and its recent translation into English (Tapia 2016b; Zavaleta 2016) will further galvanise scholarship exploring and excavating his work. On an empirical note, the analysis presented here—limited as it has been by space—has only been able to offer a preliminary sketch of the interwoven processes of capital accumulation, state formation, nation-building and the development of historic blocs. Each of these processes has yet to be fully fleshed out, and a lot of work remains to be done on the interplay between them, something that, more often than not, is overlooked. The confusion identified at the start of the chapter, as it were, still reigns. This is one of the outstanding tasks required if we are to fully comprehend the limitations of Evo Morales' time in power and fully grapple with the manner of his demise.

Notes

1 *Ayni* is the distribution of communal labour through a system of the direct return of favours and *mink'a* is the demonstration of solidarity with the community through collaboration on a communal project.
2 Interpellation is an Althusserian concept which captures ideological 'hailing' and focuses on 'subjectivity rather than subjection' (Freeland 2016: 278).
3 This organic relationship with the MAS is *only* with these sectors and does not extend, as Eduardo Silva (2018) claims, to all social organisations.
4 Nonetheless, as discussed below, support for Morales in the popular economy was by no means guaranteed, and the formation of an emergent petty bourgeoisie with middle-class aspirations undermined some of his support in later years.
5 For a more detailed analysis of how this dynamic played out, see McNelly (2020c)
6 Symptomatic of the weakness of social organisations aligned with the MAS were the actions of the Central Obrera Boliviana (COB) during this period, which flip-flopped around without any sense of political spine. Having called for Morales to step down on 10 November, in the face of extreme violence a week later it suggested that this was a massive mistake, and was subsequently, following this fatal indecision, virtually absent from the political scene for the rest of the crisis.

7 My point about employment opportunities needs qualification, as the size of the state bureaucracy did increase three-fold under Morales (see Soruco 2015; Soruco, Franco, and Durán 2014). However, these posts were often assigned by political means, favouring MAS-affiliated social organisations and prominent MAS supporters.

8 This is to say nothing of the thousands, possibly millions, of people who have migrated from rural Bolivia to other parts of the world, most notably Buenos Aires, Argentina, São Paulo, Brazil and Madrid, Spain (see Ikemura Amaral 2018).

9 I make this argument in more detail in (McNelly, 2020a).

10 For more on the Katarismo movement, see Albó (1987) and Hurtado (2016).

11 The Unity Pact was comprised of CONAMAQ, CIDOB, the CSUTSB, Las Bartolinas, the women's wing of the CSUTCB, the colonist settlers' union, the landless peasants movement, the Assembly of the Guaraní People, the Block of Indigenous and Peasant Organizations of the Northern Amazon and the Salaried Workers' Union of Santa Cruz (Garcés, 2011: 49).

12 'Camba', a term thought to have originated from the Guaraní word for friend, was first used to describe peasants and was synonymous with the peons tied to large *haciendas* through debt. Over time, it came to encompass both peasants and landowners from the eastern part of the country (Stearman 1985: 20).

13 For more detail, see Gustafson (2006) and Plata (2008).

Bibliography

Albó, Xavier. 1987. "From MNRistas to Kataristas to Katari." In *Resistance, Rebellion and Consciousness in the Andean Peasant World, 18th to 20th Centuries*, edited by Steve Stern. 379–419. Wisconsin: University of Wisconsin Press.

ANF. 2019. "Evo Advierte Que Sufrirá Un 'Golpe de Estado' Si Gana Las Elecciones." Página Siete. October 14, 2019. https://www.paginasiete.bo/nacional/2019/10/14/evo-advierte-que-sufrira-un-golpe-de-estado-si-gana-las-elecciones-234268.html.

Arze, Carlos, and Felix Maita Pérez. 2000. *Empleos y Condiciones Laborales En Bolivia: 1989–1992–1995*. La Paz: CEDLA.

Bautista, Rafael. 2011. "Hacia Una Constitución Del Sentido Significativo Del 'Vivir Bien.'" In *Vivir Bien: ¿Paradigma No Capitalista?*, edited by Ivonne Farah H and Luciano Vasapollo, 93–122. La Paz: CIDES-UMSA and Plural editores.

Braga, Ruy. 2019. "From the Union Hall to the Church." Jacobin. July 4, 2019. https://www.jacobinmag.com/2019/04/bolsonaro-election-unions-labor-evangelical-churches.

Braudel, Fernand, and Immanuel Wallerstein. 2009. "History and the Social Sciences: The Longue Durée." *Review (Fernand Braudel Centre)* 32 (2): 171–203.

Castañón, Enrique. 2017. *Empresas Transnacionales En El Agronegocio Soyero: Una Aproximación a Sus Estrategias y Relaciones Con Los Pequeños Productores*. La Paz: Fundación TIERRA.

Chávez V., Fernando. 2019. "Según La Encuesta, 68% Cree Que Habrá Fraude Electoral." Página Siete. September 29, 2019. https://www.paginasiete.bo/nacional/2019/9/29/segun-la-encuesta-68-cree-que-habra-fraude-electoral-232481.html.

Dunkerley, James. 2013. "Bolivia En Ese Entonces: Bolivia, Hoy Revisitado 30 Años Después." *Revista Boliviana de Investigación* 10 (1): 191–212.

ECLAC. 2017. *Economic Survey of Latin America and the Caribbean 2017.* Santiago: United Nations Economic Commission for Latin America and the Caribbean.

———. 2019a. *Economic Survey of Latin America and the Caribbean 2019: The New Global Financial Context: Effects and Transmission Mechanisms in the Region.* Santiago de Chile: ECLAC.

———. 2019b. *Preliminary Overview of the Economies of Latin America and the Caribbean 2019.* Santiago de Chile: ECLAC.

Freeland, Anne. 2016. "Afterward." In *Towards a History of the National Popular in Bolivia, 1879–1980*, 272–285. Chicago: Seagull Books.

———. 2019. "The National-Popular in Bolivia: History, Crisis and Social Knowledge." *Postcolonial Studies* 22 (3): 275–282.

Galindo, María. 2020. "Kristallnacht in Bolivia." In *Towards Freedom's Bolivia Reader: Voices on the Political and Social Crisis*, edited by Dawn Marie Paley, 21–26. Mexico City: Towards Freedom.

Garcés, Fernando. 2011. "The Domestication of Indigenous Autonomies in Bolivia: From the Pact of Unity to the New Constitution." In *Remapping Bolivia: Resources, Territory and Indigeneity in a Plurinational State*, edited by Bret Gustafson and Nicole Fabricant, 46–67. Santa Fe: School for Advanced Research Press.

Gill, Lesley. 1994. *Precarious Dependencies: Gender, Class, and Domestic Service in Bolivia.* New York: Columbia University Press.

Gudynas, Eduardo. 2012. "Estado Compensador y Nuevos Extractivismos." *Nueva Sociedad* 237: 128–146.

Gustafson, Bret. 2006. "Spectacles of Autonomy and Crisis: Or, What Bulls and Beauty Queens Have to Do with Regionalism in Eastern Bolivia." *Journal of Latin American Anthropology* 11 (2): 351–379.

———. 2016. "Bolivia After the 'No' Vote." NACLA. March 7, 2016. https://nacla.org/news/2016/03/07/bolivia-after-no-vote.

Gutiérrez, Raquel. 2020. "Upheaval in Bolivia Lurches Towards Disaster." In *Towards Freedom's Bolivia Reader: Voices on the Political and Social Crisis*, edited by Dawn Marie Paley, 7–12. Mexico City: Towards Freedom.

Haarstad, Håvard. 2014. "Cross-Scalar Dynamics of the Resource Curse: Constraints on Local Participation in the Bolivian Gas Sector." *Journal of Development Studies* 50 (7): 977–990.

Horn, Philipp. 2018. "Emerging Urban Indigenous Spaces in Bolivia: A Combined Planetary and Postcolonial Perspective." In *Emerging Urban Spaces: A Planetary Perspective*, edited by Philipp Horn et al, 43–64. New York: Springer (The Urban Book Series).

Hurtado, Javier. 2016. *El Katarismo.* La Paz: Centro de investigacion social.

Hylton, Forrest, and Jeffery R. Webber. 2019. "The Eighteenth Brumaire of Macho Camacho: Jeffery R. Webber (with Forrest Hylton) on the Coup in Bolivia." Verso Blog. October 15, 2019. https://www.versobooks.com/blogs/4493-the-eighteenth-brumaire-of-macho-camacho-jeffery-r-webber-with-forrest-hylton-on-the-coup-in-bolivia.

Ikemura Amaral, Aiko. 2018. "Identity, Work, and Mobility among Bolivian Market Vendors in El Alto and São Paulo." The University of Essex.

ILO. 2017. "2017 Labour Overview: Latin America and the Caribbean." Lima.

INE. 2012. "Censo Nacional de Población y Vivienda 2012." La Paz.

———. 2020. "Instituto Nacional de Estadística." 2020. http://www.ine.gob.bo/.

Kaup, B. Z. 2010. "A Neoliberal Nationalization?: The Constraints on Natural-Gas-Led Development in Bolivia." *Latin American Perspectives* 37 (3): 123–138.

Lagos Rojas, Felipe. 2018. "Thinking with Zavaleta: Projecting Lo Abigarrado onto Neoliberal Globalization." In *Latin American Marxisms in Context: Past and Present*, edited by Peter Baker, Irina Feldman, Mike Geddes, Felipe Lagos, and Roberto Pareja, 133–153. Newcastle upon Tyne: Cambridge Scholars Publishing.

Lizárraga, Paulo. 2019. "Conade Llama a Cabildo Nacional y Vigilias En Defensa Del Voto." Página Siete. October 21, 2019. https://www.paginasiete.bo/nacional/2019/10/21/conade-llama-cabildo-nacional-vigilias-en-defensa-del-voto-235078.html.

Marx, Karl. 1977. *A Contribution to the Critique of Political Economy*. Moscow: Progress Publishers.

———. 1978. "The Eighteenth Brumaire of Louis Bonaparte." *The Marx-Engels Reader*, no. March 1852: 594–617.

———. 1982. *Capital: A Critique of Political Economy Volume 1*. Harmondsworth: Penguin Books.

McKay, Ben M. 2018. "The Politics of Agrarian Change in Bolivia's Soy Complex." *Journal of Agrarian Change* 18 (2): 406–424.

McNeish, John-Andrew. 2013. "Extraction, Protest and Indigeneity in Bolivia: The TIPNIS Effect." *Latin American and Caribbean Ethnic Studies* 8 (2): 221–242.

McNelly, Angus. 2016. "Evo Morales and the Limits to 21st Century Socialism." *ROAR Magazine*, March 2016.

———. 2019. "Bolivia in Crisis: How Evo Morales Was Forced Out." The Conversation. 2019. https://theconversation.com/bolivia-in-crisis-how-evo-morales-was-forced-out-126859?fbclid=IwAR1OAZIfWTuQ6AT3SUwahIeZw34x7PvkMnaYcTqe-fxCEzMX_ZKmLblIA_I.

———. 2020a. "Baroque Modernity in Latin America: Situating Indigeneity, Urban Indigeneity and the Popular Economy." *Bulletin of Latin American Research* 00 (0): 0–0.

———. 2020b. "Neostructuralism and Its Class Character in the Political Economy of Bolivia under Evo Morales." *New Political Economy* 25 (3): 419–438.

———. 2020c. "The Incorporation of Social Organizations under the MAS in Bolivia." *Latin American Perspectives* 47 (4): 76–95.

Mendes Loureiro, Pedro. 2018. "Reformism, Class Conciliation and the Pink Tide: Material Gains and Their Limits." In *The Social Life of Economic Inequalities in Contemporary Latin America*, edited by Margit Ystanes and Iselin Åsedotter Strønen, 35–56. Basingstoke: Palgrave Macmillan.

Nuñez del Prado, José. 2009. *Economías Indígenas. Estados Del Arte Desde Bolivia y La Economía Política*. La Paz: CIDES-DIPGIS-ASDI.

Paley, Dawn Marie. 2020. *Toward Freedom's Bolivia Reader: Voices on the Political and Social Crisis Following the October 2019 Elections in Bolivia.* Mexico City: Towards Freedom.

Plata, Wilfredo. 2008. "El Discurso Autonomista de Las Élites de Santa Cruz." In *Los Barones Del Oriente: El Poder En Santa Cruz Ayer y Hoy*, edited by Ximena Soruco et al, 101–172. Santa Cruz: Fundación TIERRA.

Postero, Nancy Grey. 2017. *The Indigenous State: Race, Politics and Performance in Plurinational Bolivia.* Berkeley: University of California Press.

Powęska, Radoslaw. 2013. *Indigenous Movements and Building the Plurinational State in Bolivia: Organisation and Identity in the Trajectory of the CSUTCB and CONAMAQ.* Warsaw: CESLA UW.

Rao, Rahul. 2017. "Recovering Reparative Readings of Postcolonialism and Marxism." *Critical Sociology* 43 (4–5): 587–598.

Rivera, Silvia. 1996. "Trabajo de Mujer: Explotación Capitalista y Opresión Colonial Entre Las Migrantes Aymaras de La Paz y El Alto, Bolivia." In *Ser Mujer Indígena, Chola o Birlocha En La Bolivia Postcolonial de Los Años 90*, edited by Silvia Rivera, 163–300. La Paz: Ministerio de Desarrollo Humano.

Rutazibwa, Olivia Umurerwa, and Robbie Shilliam. 2018. "Postcolonial Politics: An Introduction." In *Routledge Handbook of Postcolonial Politics*, edited by Olivia U. Rutazibwa and Robbie Shilliam, 16–32. Abingdon and New York: Routledge.

Salazar, Huáscar. 2015. *Se Han Adueñado El Proceso de Lucha: Horizontes Comunitario-Populares En Tensión y La Reconstitución de La Dominación En La Bolivia Del MAS.* Cochabamba: SOCEE y Autodeterminación.

Schavelzon, Salvador. 2015. *Plurinacionalidad y Vivir Bien/Buen Vivir.* Buenos Aires: CLACSO.

Silva, Eduardo. 2018. "Social Movements and the Second Incorporation in Bolivia and Ecuador." In *Reshaping the Political Arena in Latin America: From Resisting Neoliberalism to the Second Incorporation*, edited by Eduardo Silva and Federico M. Rossi, 32–59. Pittsburgh: University of Pittsburgh Press.

Soruco, Ximena. 2011. "El Porvenir, the Future That Is No Longer Possible." In *Remapping Bolivia: Resources, Territory and Indigeneity in a Plurinational State*, edited by Nicole Fabricant and Bret Gustafson, 68–90. Santa Fe: School for Advanced Research Press.

———. 2015. "La Nueva Burocracia Plurinacional En Bolivia: Entre La Democratización y La Institucionalización." *Nueva Sociedad* 257.

Soruco, Ximena, Daniela Franco, and Mariela Durán. 2014. *Composición Social Del Estado Plurinacional: Hacia Descolonización de La Burocracia.* La Paz: Centro de investigacion social.

Stearman, Allyn MacLean. 1985. *Camba and Kolla: Migration and Development in Santa Cruz, Bolivia.* Orlando: University of Florida Press.

Tapia, Luis. 2002. *La Producción Del Conocimiento Local. Historia y Política En La Obra de René Zavaleta.* La Paz: Muela del Diablo Editores.

———. 2016a. *El Momento Constitutivo Del Estado Moderno Capitalista En Bolivia.* La Paz: CIDES-UMSA.

———. 2016b. *The Production of Local Knowledge: History and Politics in the Work of René Zavaleta Mercado*. Edited by Alison Spedding. Chicago: Seagull Books.
———. 2019. "History and Structure in the Thought of René Zavaleta." *Historical Materialism* 27 (3): 127–135.
Tassi, Nico, Carmen Medeiros, Antonio Rodríguez-Carmona, and Giovana Ferrufino. 2013. *Hacer Plata Sin Plata: El Desborde de Los Comerciantes Populares En Bolivia*. La Paz: PIEB.
Thomson, Sinclair. 2019. "Self-Knowledge and Self-Determination at the Limits of Capitalism: Introduction to René Zavaleta Mercado's towards a History of the National-Popular in Bolivia: 1879–1980." *Historical Materialism* 27 (3): 83–98.
Unidad, Pacto de. 2006. "Propuesta Para La Nueva Constitución Política Del Estado." In *Horizontes de La Asamblea Constituyente*, edited by Raúl Prada Alcoreza, 167–206. La Paz: Ediciones Yachaywasi.
Véliz, Juan Carlos. 2016. "Indígenas a Evo: Usted Menosprecia Nuestra Capacidad de Razonamiento Sobre El Bala – Diario Pagina Siete." Página Siete. 2016. http://www.paginasiete.bo/nacional/2016/11/17/indigenas-evo-usted-menosprecia-nuestra-capacidad-razonamiento-sobre-bala-117314.html.
Webber, Jeffery R. 2011a. *From Rebellion to Reform in Bolivia: Class Struggle, Indigenous Liberation, and the Politics of Evo Morales*. Chicago: Haymarket Books.
———. 2011b. *Red October: Left-Indigenous Struggles in Modern Bolivia*. Chicago and London: Haymarket Books.
———. 2016. "Evo Morales and the Political Economy of Passive Revolution in Bolivia, 2006–2015." *Third World Quarterly* 37 (10): 1855–1876.
Wikileaks. 2015. *The Wikileak Files*. London and New York: Verso.
Wolff, Jonas. 2016. "Business Power and the Politics of Postneoliberalism: Relations between Governments and Economic Elites in Bolivia and Ecuador." *Latin American Politics and Society* 58 (2): 124–147.
World Bank. 2020. "Población Urbana (% Del Total) – Bolivia | Data." World Bank. 2020. https://datos.bancomundial.org/indicador/SP.URB.TOTL.IN.ZS?end=2018&locations=BO&start=2000.
Zavaleta, René. 1982. "Problemas de La Determinación Dependiente y La Forma Primordial." In *America Latina: Desarrollo y Perspectivas Democráticas*, edited by Francisco Rojas Aravena, 55–84. San José: Ediciones FLASCO.
———. 2008. *Lo National-Popular En Bolivia*. La Paz: Plural editores.
———. 2013a. "El Estado En América Latina." In *Obra Completa. René Zavaleta Mercado (Tomo II: Ensayos 1975–1984)*, edited by Mauricio Souza Crespo, 611–636. La Paz: Plural editores.
———. 2013b. "Las Masas En Noviembre." In *Obra Completa. René Zavaleta Mercado (Tomo II: Ensayos 1975–1984)*, edited by Mauricio Souza Crespo, 97–142. La Paz: Plural editores.
———. 2016. *Towards a History of the National-Popular in Bolivia*. Edited by Anne Freeland. Chicago: Seagull Books.
Zibechi, Raúl. 2020. "Evo's Fall, the Fascist Right, & the Power of Memory." In *Towards Freedom's Bolivia Reader: Voices on the Political and Social Crisis*, edited by Dawn Marie Paley, 30–35. Mexico City: Towards Freedom.

4 Continuity and change in Bolivian land politics and policy

Bret Gustafson

Introduction

This chapter is an overview of the main issues shaping contemporary political struggles over land in Bolivia. The chapter draws on the work of Bolivian researchers with a focus on continuities and potential changes before and after the tumultuous political upheaval of 2019 and 2020. The chapter critically engages the legacies of the government of Evo Morales and sketches out the primary areas of conflict that Bolivian activists and movements are facing going forward. The chapter begins with a general context and traces land policy during the government of Evo Morales, illustrating a shift from a more progressive approach to land reform (roughly 2006 to 2012) toward a conciliatory arrangement with eastern Bolivia's agro-industrial elite (from 2013 to 2019). Four areas are examined in more detail: gender and land; the battle over GMOs, the fires in the Amazon, and Indigenous territorial autonomies. I then turn to the political upheaval of 2019 and 2020. When Evo Morales was forced to resign in November of 2019, an interim government took over that was by and large a direct representative of the agro-industrial elite of the east. I describe various ways that the interim government used the capture of the state to further advance the interests of wealthy landowners. I conclude by considering how the return of the MAS in November of 2020 may or may not bring a return to progressive land policy.

General context

Bolivia's population was mostly rural until the mid-1980s, but this rural to urban migration accelerated further in the 1990s and 2000s. Economic growth, albeit concentrated in urban areas, attracted more migrants, with Bolivia in 2020 being about 70% urban. But a relatively high proportion of 30% of the country still lives in the rural area.[1] About 54% of the rural population lives in poverty, with 35% in extreme poverty (CEPAL 2019; Mamani 2020a). In the Andes, lands are simply too scarce to sustain new generations. Combined with climate change, water scarcity and soil erosion – as well as the impacts of mining in some regions – rural survival has become challenging in much of the highlands (Mamani 2020a). In eastern Bolivia, the expansion of large-scale agro-industry has occupied significant swaths of land. Despite some new rural settlements and land titles granted to smallholders, rural communities still struggle to get access to credits and inputs, and often end up sending new generations to the city or abandoning the land. Yet urban life is increasingly equally challenging, given the high levels of un- and under-employment. Andean migration to eastern Bolivia has long offered a safety valve, yet increasingly the availability of new land is limited both by local opposition and the spread of agro-industry.

In eastern Bolivia, the most economically productive lands are increasingly monopolized by large-scale agro-industries, mostly producing for export. Researchers from Fundación Tierra estimate that of the 3 million hectares of arable land in Bolivia, 1.3 million are planted in soy and around 700,000 in corn, sugar cane, rice, or wheat, most of that controlled by big agro-industries. The remainder, around 1 million hectares, produces most of what the country eats. Land inequality is high. About 800 large landowners have holdings of 5,000 hectares or more, while 787,000 small producers have holdings of 50 hectares or less. In the case of soy, the inequality is dramatic. Of the large producers, 2% control 70% of the land, a handful (20%) have mid-size properties of less than 1,000 hectares, and 78% are smallholders, with less than 50 hectares (Fundación Tierra 2020). This creates what has been called a dual structure in the land. On one side, there is large-scale capital-intensive agro-industry, focused primarily on soy and cattle, and to a lesser extent sugar cane, much of it destined for export. On the other side are food-producing smaller holders producing for the domestic market. Recent years have seen the expansion of small- and medium-scale farms producing for the market as well, especially in the regions of settlements north of Santa Cruz and in emerging alternative crops, such as quinoa, as well as coca, fruits, vegetables, and others. Yet even with this tripartite structure, a highly unequal distribution of land and agrarian power persists even in the wake of 14 years of the presumably progressive agrarian policies of Evo Morales (Colque et al. 2016). If the urban economy is not able to absorb labor, the country will need to do more to create economic opportunities for rural communities, which will require challenging the expansion of the agro-industrial elite.

The unfinished agrarian revolution

Evo Morales, elected in 2005, launched a new agrarian reform in 2006 that promised just such a challenge. Prior land reforms, after the 1952 Revolution, and then again in 1996, had distributed some land to small farmers, but were ultimately limited in their effects and did not address deeper structures of inequality. The 1996 reform, aimed more at creating conditions for a free market in land than in pursuing social justice, initiated a limited process of land distribution and Indigenous territorial demarcation. But in both cases, large land-owning elites appropriated the legal measures to consolidate their hold on ill-gotten lands or to prevent more radical forms of redistribution. The law passed by the Morales government in 2006 was more ambitious. It set criteria for "socio-economic" function, such that lands held for speculation or farms exploiting workers through debt peonage could be expropriated by the government. It stopped the auctioning off of public lands and established collective titling for Indigenous and peasant farmers, meaning that any distribution of state lands would no longer go to the wealthy. Finally, it allowed for the participation of peasant and Indigenous organizations in the process and gave the state more power to intervene. In short, it was indeed a "redirection" of the agrarian reform (Colque et al. 2016:215).

The effort was marked by the redistribution of publicly owned land, titling of Indigenous territories, and cadastral "cleaning up" (*saneamiento*) of contested claims. In parts of the country, the MAS used the land reform to advance Indigenous and peasant claims, often leveraging these against particularly troublesome political opponents (Gustafson 2020a). It was a conquest of the government that saw almost 85% of the country's land "*saneado*" (with clear titles). A significant portion of the land that was redistributed went to Indigenous Peoples and small farmers. For example, over 50% of the land titled by 2014, almost 23 million hectares, were for the Indigenous "communitarian lands" (*tierras comunitarias de orígen* [TCO]), territorial conquests of years of struggle (Colque et al. 2016:185).

Yet the government of Evo Morales, although voicing a seemingly radical language of land reform and Indigenous rights, ultimately demobilized more radical demands for land and abandoned significant efforts to limit the amount of land held by the latifundists. As it sought to defend its hegemony, it redirected peasant political mobilization into state patronage rather than challenges to agrarian inequality. In addition, while the MAS had backed land occupations by peasant organizations, these radical efforts were eventually brought to a halt. There were also internal schisms. Many peasant organizations – primarily migrants from the Andes, or their descendants – wanted individual or family titles. Most Indigenous organizations, those largely in the eastern lowlands who shared a different agrarian history not characterized by insertion into commercial production, supported collective territories. The schism led to conflicts within the Morales government, which gradually sidelined supporters of collective Indigenous territories (Gustafson 2020a). Indigenous organizations had hoped to transform the TCOs into autonomous territories, but the new constitution limited Indigenous autonomies to existing municipal jurisdictions, and only to those where Indigenous peoples could muster a majority vote to convert them to autonomous municipalities (Garcés 2011). At this writing, there are only three out of over 300 municipalities in the country. In addition, the TCOs were not largely in economically productive lands and remain partly occupied by third-party (non-Indigenous) smallholders. In terms of large-scale expropriation of latifundias, this never really happened. Most lands redistributed were government lands. Many private holdings that should have been expropriated – due to their illegality or because they did not fulfill a socio-economic function – were left untouched (and, as below, granted more time to try to certify that they were actually productive). Evo Morales's election challenged the absolute power of the eastern Bolivia agrarian elite, but it did not dismantle it. In fact, by 2010 or so, the Morales government began to make concessions to the agrarian elite in a bid for political stability. This included, paradoxically, increased titling of lands to those who were not poor peasants or Indigenous peoples and, as above, a general halt to more radical efforts to expropriate land that was not fulfilling a social and economic good (one of the criteria established in the 2006 law). The government approach to land shifted from a revolutionary stance to one that seemed focused on appeasing large landowners and using the land reform office to expand the patronage networks of the government (McKay 2018).

Gender and land

Despite the recent improvement of the economic indices in Bolivia, a significant sector of the population continues to live in poverty. Of this group, those who continue trying to eke out a living on rural small-holdings include a significant population of around 1.6 million women in the Andes. Because men often migrate to the city, leaving behind the women in the communities, researchers have referred to a "feminization of the rural," which, by extension equates to a feminization of rural poverty (Mamani 2020a). For decades, scholars have argued that one of the fundamental issues of gender inequality in Latin America revolves around unequal access to land for women (Deere and León 2001). It has been argued that land ownership is not only a key to subsistence but is also tied to political subjecthood (Lastarria-Cornhiel 2009). Traditional forms of collective ownership, such as the ayllu in the Andes, or non-privatized customary use of the commons may have allowed for more equitable access for women. Yet collective titling can just as easily marginalize women – or pit women's interests against Indigenous interests (Deere and León 2001). At any rate, once privatized regimes of individualized land ownership were established, the impact has been to deepen gender inequality because individual titles were largely written in the name of the male as the head of household. In this way, even ostensibly revolutionary projects of land reform could cement male power further. Such was the case of the 1952 Land Reform in Bolivia, which established individual ownership through male heads of household and organized peasant unions (*sindicatos*) to mediate relations between land, communities, and the state. The ayllu form persisted in some areas, but male title-holding and the *sindicato* structure cemented deeply patriarchal forms of state politics onto Andean life. Furthermore, over time, individual land-holdings were increasingly subdivided among heirs, leading to out-migration and the phenomenon known as "minifundia" – families whose land consists merely of tiny plots or rows of land that do not allow for subsistence.

With the neoliberal era voicing the discourse of "gender equality" fit into a liberal model of market-oriented reform, the issue of co-ownership (joint titling) was introduced in the 1996 land reform legislation, the so-called Ley INRA (*Instituto Nacional de Reforma Agraria*). Deere and León (2001) argue that the so-called "engendering" of neoliberal land reform was largely aimed at legitimating a broader process of market-oriented policies and establishing formal legal equality for women and men. Yet, as they did elsewhere, neoliberal economic policies did not produce substantive equality. In the case of Bolivia, neoliberal reforms ushered in a period of growing poverty and inequality that did little to redistribute real structural or economic power to the poor, much less to women (Farthing and Kohl 2006). Furthermore, while the neoliberal INRA Law set out the criteria of gender equality, it did not mandate joint titling or establish firm procedures for pursuing it, such that it came down to decisions made by land functionaries and communities at the moment titles were written up – spaces largely dominated by men. The INRA process did little to inform women of their rights or train its own personnel in the issues of gender equality in titling. Other challenges, including illiteracy, lack of state IDs, and the functionaries' lack of knowledge of Indigenous languages also limited women's participation (Lastarria-Cornhiel 2009:2016–2018; 224). The main goals of the 1996 reform were to encourage the formation of a free market in land, not to redistribute land or power to women and the poor. By the time INRA began to rethink its approach to gender, the entire neoliberal project had begun to collapse.[2]

The 2006 Agrarian Reform law passed under Evo Morales sought to address this in part by implementing joint titling more forcefully. What this meant is that the historical pattern of titling lands only in the name of men, as the head of the family, would be transformed such that all titles for nuclear families were to be written as co-owned by women and men. The process had a significant impact. Of the 2.1 million beneficiaries of land titling tied to the reform, about 46% are women (Mamani 2020b). As such, almost a million women are now recognized as full or joint owners of land. Although women have gained some access to legal titles, there is still much more to be done to translate this ownership (or joint ownership) into effective power. In some areas, women were titled marginal or unproductive lands. In political organizations, women are often excluded and women remain subject to high levels of domestic violence. There are notable exceptions, of course, such as the women's branch of the national peasant movement, known as the "Bartolinas" (*Confederación Nacional de Mujeres Campesinas Indígenas Originarios de Bolivia "Bartolina Sisa"*), which has been an influential political actor. Many women from this organization took prominent roles in the MAS government. Yet challenges remain. During the MAS government, several initiatives aimed at addressing these issues were implemented, with uneven success. These included laws aimed at curbing domestic violence, racial and gender discrimination, and sexual harassment. Nonetheless, implementation challenges in rural areas, along with some community opposition from male leaders, has limited their reach. Despite more parity for women in urban political spaces, including at the national level, the need for more assertive agrarian policies to ensure legal security, support rural agrarian projects for rural women, and secure women's roles as political administrators of their lands is clear (Mamani 2020a, 2020b).

GMOs: the roots of fascism?

The global consolidation of transnational corporations seeking to control agrarian production by way of genetically modified seeds – known colloquially as GMOs (genetically modified organisms) – is worrisome. Six companies have merged to form three giants – Bayer/Monsanto and Dow/DuPont (of the USA), and ChemChina/Syngenta (of China). While these corporations market GMOs as improved seeds necessary for human survival, GMOs are not just seeds, they are a socio-technological and economic apparatus that relies on dangerous chemical inputs and which by virtue of GMOs' material dependence on specific legal and political arrangements of power, tends to deepen economic and political inequalities. GMO seeds are programmed to be treated with toxic herbicides like glyphosate and others, chemicals sold and controlled by the seed companies themselves (Colque 2020). The same companies, through local subsidiaries, buy the products (soy in the case of Bolivia) and export them, exercising control over virtually the entire chain of supply, production, and commercialization. This involves chemical subordination and dependence, economic domination, and the expatriation of profits which accrue to those who control the rights to seeds, chemicals, and outputs.

The history of GMO expansion in Bolivia dates to 1998, when Monsanto, the global agribusiness giant, began pressuring Bolivia to allow the introduction of its GMO soy called "RR" (or RR1). RR was resistant to glyphosate, a weed-killer also manufactured by Monsanto, as Roundup, a chemical identified by the World Health Organization as a probable carcinogen (IARC 2016). Because of opposition from environmental organizations and others, Monsanto failed to introduce it into Bolivia legally. But RR soy entered the country illegally and its use spread, creating a de facto and growing dependence. Finally, under immense pressure from big agro-industry, RR soy was finally made legal during the tumultuous period of the Carlos Mesa government that followed the massive uprisings of 2003 and the ouster of the neoliberal President Gonzalo Sánchez de Lozada. When vice-president Mesa took over, he found himself pressured by the eastern Bolivian agrarian elite and was vying for their support. In his last days as President, a ministerial resolution was signed that approved RR1 soy. When Mesa resigned and Eduardo Rodríguez Veltzé became president in April of 2005, that resolution was raised to the level of a supreme decree. GMO soy had arrived (Molina 2020).

GMO soy gradually displaced conventional soy entirely. Yet as weeds became resistant to glyphosate, it became clear that RR was no miracle seed. Outputs began dropping after a few years (based on figures by Gonzalo Colque in Fundación Tierra 2020). In addition, the soy industry hoped to expand into the drier lands of the Chiquitano forest. The transnational firms with a presence in Bolivia are now pushing two new GMO soy varieties: HB4 and Intacta. HB4, with a gene from sunflowers, is supposedly drought resistant and has genes to protect against both glyphosates, and a new herbicide called glufosinate (*glufosinato de amonio*). Glufosinate has already been banned in France for its toxic risks. Intacta is supposedly resistant to both glyphosate and certain insects and both are said to be more productive than RR (Molina 2020). Yet during the early years of the MAS government, characterized by environmentalist rhetoric in defense of the *Pachamama,* or Mother Earth, there were no more openings to GMO soy. Yet as the more progressive period of agrarian reform gave way to the conciliatory turn to the agro-industrial elite (and gas revenues started declining), the MAS began to make moves aimed at expanding the agricultural frontier in the east. In part, the argument was that this would aim to increase biofuel production. The idea was to replace imported diesel fuel, a key input for the agro-industrial sector itself that had long been subsidized by the state. Biodiesel produced from soy and ethanol produced from sugar were seen as an answer to fossil fuel dependency that would also encourage more agricultural production. Yet RR soy was no longer productive and the big farmers wanted the new seeds. Again, using a supreme decree (see Table 4.1),

Table 4.1 Major legal actions affecting land use in Bolivia, 2005–2020

Interim Governments of Carlos Mesa and Eduardo Rodríguez Veltzé (2003–2005) the last days of 'neoliberalism'	
DS 28225 July 1, 2005	Authorization of the use of GMO soy (RR, glyphosate resistant)
Law 3207 September 30, 2005	Five-year tax holiday to promote biodiesel production
Evo Morales and the MAS (2006–2011) *the unfinished agrarian revolution*	
Law 3545 November 28, 2006	Redirection of the Agrarian Reform; some expropriations and redistribution of land
New Constitution February 7, 2009	New constitution with limited Indigenous autonomies; prohibits import of GMOs
Law 144 June 26, 2011	Prohibited introduction of GMO seeds that threatened Bolivian biodiversity (i.e. corn); required identification of GMO-based food & seed imports; also called for procedures to control "production, importation, and commercialization" of GMO products

Evo Morales and the MAS (2012–2019) *the opening to the agro-industrial elite*	
Law 337/2013	Replaced penal sanctions for illegal deforestation between 1996 and 2011 with small fines
Law 502/2014	Extended the reduced fines for illegal deforestation
Law 739/2015	Extended the reduced fines for illegal deforestation through 2017
Law 740/2015	Five-year extension for large landowners to verify their socio-economic function
Law 741/2015	Allowed for limited deforestation in areas zoned for forest protection
Law 1098/2018	Law to promote biodiesel production and its purchase by the state
DS 3874 April 18, 2019	Established "abbreviated procedures" for two new soy gmos (HB4 & INTACTA) for biodiesel production
Law 1178/2019	Forgiveness for unauthorized burning
DS 3973/2019	Allowed for controlled burning and expansion of agricultural frontier in lands zoned for forest in Beni
Jeanine Añez Interim Government (2019–2020) *state capture by the agro-industrial elite*	
DS 4232 May 7, 2020	Established "shortened procedures" for evaluating introduction of GMO corn, sugar cane, cotton, wheat and soy
DS 4238 May 14, 2020	Ordered the National Committee on Biosecurity to approve the procedures for the new GMO seeds
DS4348 October 23, 2020	Called for the identification of areas for the use of GMO corn
Inauguration of Luís Arce, Return of the MAS government (Nov. 8, 2020- ?)	

Sources: CEDIB (2020); Villalobos (2020); Molina (2020).

the government of Evo Morales moved to accelerate approval of HB4 and Intacta, just a few months before the chaotic November 2019 elections. Nonetheless, the 2009 Constitution states in one article that the "production, importation, and commercialization of [GMOs] will be regulated by law," suggesting that a presidential decree was insufficient to make such a change. And, somewhat contradictorily, another article in the Constitution "prohibits the importation, production, and commercialization of [GMOs] and toxic elements that damage health and the environment" (cited in Molina 2020). Reflecting the conflicted negotiations between the social movements and agribusinesses that marked the writing of the constitution, from either perspective Morales's pro-GMO decree is unconstitutional. These contradictions are also reflected in Bolivia's 2011 Law 144 on the "Communitarian and Agroindustrial Productive Revolution" (see Table 4.1). The law both prohibited GMO seeds that threatened Bolivia's natural biodiversity but also called for procedures for the import and sale of other GMO products. With the TIPNIS conflict and this contradictory approach, the turn toward the agro-industrial elite continued. By late 2019, Evo Morales himself had been ousted and was in exile in Argentina. I return to GMOs and the coup government that followed below.

The paradox of all of this in the Bolivian case is that large-scale agro-industry in eastern Bolivia is, economically speaking, unprofitable and nonsensical, working against human welfare and nature. Once GMO soy expands, given its dependence on toxic herbicides like glyphosate, other crops can no longer grow in the same region, not to mention the risks for human health and the contamination of soil and water. Soy from Bolivia is shipped to Peru and Colombia, and returned as finished products (oil and processed foods). Despite the marketing tactics of the multinationals, it does not contribute to food security or food sovereignty. Nor does large-scale agriculture employ much labor. The wider process of soy expansion and mechanization actually tends to reduce the need for labor, displacing smaller farmers and creating surplus populations who have little alternative but to migrate to the city (McKay and Colque 2016; McKay 2018).

This exclusionary push combines with the domination of those smaller or medium-size farmers who remain as providers of soy to the buyers. Smaller landholders who participate in the soy industry are invariably trapped in debt relations that force their continued dependence on seeds and chemical inputs. It is for this reason that the agro-industrial elite is often able to mobilize some smaller growers to support their push for GMOs (and likely partially explains the MAS overtures to this sector as well). Yet the system tends to keep smaller growers trapped in debt and moves wealth upwards. The model tends to exacerbate land inequality by concentrating larger and larger landholdings into fewer hands. The agro-industrial sector pays very little in the way of taxes, a fraction of what other businesses are required to pay on their profits. The industry also relies on government subsidies on diesel fuel (and the government is also subsidizing biofuel production), and government-subsidized loans, often forgiven when crops fail or prices drop. Finally, and despite those who argue that GMOs are crucial for food security or food sovereignty, most of Bolivia's food production comes from smaller farmers, not from the big agro-industry, much less from GMO soy. As Gonzalo Colque argues (Fundación Tierra 2020:50), despite the fact that the entire apparatus of GMO soy is virtually unprofitable and contributes very little to the public good (actually costing the state in subsidies and bailouts), the attachment of economic interests – purveyors of chemicals, seeds, machinery, and the like – creates a network of powerful interests that defend its survival and expansion. By extension, since all of this entails a specific legal regime (laws, decrees, regulations), its expansion requires deep penetration of the state by the interests of multinational firms and their local partners, among them large landowners and business chambers. It is this convergence of anti-democratic power aimed at solidifying monopoly control – and its association with other arch-conservative ideological strands in eastern Bolivia – that have led some researchers to refer to GMOs as the expression of fascist power (Colque 2020).

Indigenous autonomies

The Indigenous movements of Bolivia have been central protagonists in the shaping of agrarian and land policy for many decades. In the 1990s, Indigenous peoples marched from the lowlands of the east to the capital at La Paz, not once, but several times, demanding territorial rights. While peasant farmers and migrants from the Andes to the lowlands have generally organized around peasant unions – and often demanded familial or individual titles – one of the central demands of Indigenous peoples has been the demarcation of collective territories. Unlike the North American context, the vocabularies of "self-determination" and "sovereignty" are not as familiar in Bolivian Indigenous languages of struggle. However, in the early 2000s, the word "autonomy" was increasingly taken up as a goal of these territorial demands (Gustafson 2009b). The ongoing struggle over land and Indigenous rights is centered around this unfinished process of territorial recovery and consolidation, as well as the configuration of some form of political self-determination that might represent a form of political, economic, and cultural autonomy within the Bolivian state.

Across Latin America autonomy has increasingly been deployed by social movements as a language for contesting various forms of power – the state, capital, large landowners, political parties – and demanding control over bodies and territories free from the exercise of multiple forms of violence, extraction, or exploitation. In Bolivia, right-wing elites have also tried to appropriate the discourse of autonomy, applying it to their demands for more regional power (Gustafson 2006, 2020b). Furthermore, the term autonomy, as elsewhere in

Latin America, also refers to institutional autonomy of certain public entities – like municipal governments or universities, who demand "autonomy" over their own budgets free from the intervention of the political party that happens to be in the seat of national power. As such, the term is laden with conflicting meanings in Bolivia, such that "Indigenous Autonomy" and what it might mean is an ongoing debate that is only slowly emerging in practice.

As pointed out above, what started as a demand for more political control over demarcated territories (the TCOs) was gradually watered down and transformed into a very limited notion of autonomy in the new constitution of 2009 (Garcés 2011). The TCOs were demarcated in ways that often cross-cut municipal boundaries, although they were not allowed to disrupt departmental boundaries. As such, TCOs were already dictated in some ways by the existing territorial order, whereas a more radical and decolonizing approach would have privileged Indigenous territorialities over existing jurisdictions. In addition, the TCOs were not given any particular economic or political powers of their own, and they remained subject to the authorities (and the budgets) of the municipalities where they happened to overlap. In some cases, the TCOs and the Indigenous population made up a large portion of the municipal space and population, such as the Guarani TCO of Charagua and Isoso. In other cases, TCOs were rural spaces minoritized within larger municipal or departmental populations. A radical approach to Indigenous autonomy might have imagined transforming all TCOs into jurisdictions of their own, but the 2009 constitution set out a series of legal hurdles that reconfirmed the existing municipal structure. Furthermore, Indigenous autonomy was only possible where a referendum vote could be had (and won) at the municipal level, such that Indigenous peoples (or rare as they might be, pro-autonomy non-indigenous allies) had to vote to transform a municipality into an "Autonomous Indigenous Territorial Entity". Wherever this happened, Indigenous peoples had the right to rewrite the municipal statutes in a way that theoretically reflected their own concepts of political order, doing away, if they desired, with mayors and councils, and implementing new forms of government, within limits. All of this had to be approved by the national constitution, setting another limit on its decolonizing potential.

While many municipalities in the Andes are largely Indigenous and could have easily voted to transform themselves into autonomous Indigenous entities, there was no great rush to change the legal structure or status. In some cases, Indigenous authorities were already in control of the municipality and many supported the MAS party. Here there emerged splits between those who wanted to pursue "autonomy" and those who sought to defend the status quo, or felt that the municipal structure was serving their needs well (Tockman 2017). In a few cases in the Andes, autonomy processes were successfully pursued, but by and large, the Indigenous Autonomous Entity is rare. In the lowlands, the situation was different. While most Indigenous organizations might have desired some form of territorial autonomy, the demographic conditions were such that winning a referendum was virtually impossible in most areas where TCOs were found. The notable exceptions were in the Guarani region, where the Guarani make up a majority in the municipality of Charagua. Charagua successfully transformed itself into an Indigenous Autonomous Entity in 2018 (Morell i Torra 2018). It remains to be seen what the longer-term impacts of this transformation might be. Of the 300-odd municipalities in the country, with around half of those potentially "Indigenous" – only about 24 municipalities are in the process of transformation. Tockman (2017) suggests that there is a kind of hybridity – with some autonomy processes closely mimicking the liberal model of existing municipal governments and others taking a more culturally varied or "communitarian" form (see also Inturias, et al., eds. 2018). For the moment, an optimistic read suggests that these municipal-level autonomies might grant more power to Indigenous peoples to determine the direction of local public investment. A warier approach might point out that this merely allows new people to access an existing system of rent-seeking – and the state budgets and revenues that that brings with it – but may not bring radical changes in daily life.

Amazon on fire?

The question of land more broadly also involves millions of hectares of forest and grassland not apt for agriculture but increasingly targeted for cattle ranching or timber cutting. Perhaps more so than other issues, the burning of forest lands has attracted intense international attention. Around August or September, farmers and ranchers burn to clear land, with fires often getting out of control. In 2019, much more than in years prior, agricultural burning was destroying vast swaths of forested areas of the Amazon basin and the dry Chiquitano forest. By 2019, the yearly burning had seemingly gotten out of control, but in fact reflected aggressive and intentional efforts by landowners to clear more agricultural land. The fires, which burned about 6.4 million hectares of vegetation, about 31% of its forests, were the largest in Bolivia's recent history (CEDIB 2020:8). A number of Bolivian NGOs, such as Centro de Documentación e Información Bolivia (CEDIB), blamed the policies of the MAS government (CEDIB 2020).

While fires have always been a yearly event, it is true that in the later 2010s the MAS government began to shore up its power in the east by making a series of legal concessions to the agro-industrial elite, some of which forgave past burning and incentivized new forest clearing. For example, in 2013 the government passed a general pardon for those who had carried out illegal deforestation between 1996 and 2011. What was once a criminal act subject to the penal code was transformed into cause for a relatively light fine. In subsequent years, the time frame was extended through the end of 2017, such that those who continued to break the law were equally absolved. On the other hand, a series of laws were passed that provided incentives to expand the agricultural frontier, while weakening protections. In 2015, another law allowed deforestation by small landholders by reducing restrictions on legal burning in areas zoned for forest maintenance (it led to burning since smaller farmers generally do not have heavy machinery to clear land). The measure, according to critics, gave way to uncontrolled burning while larger landowners took advantage of the opening to do some burning of their own. In 2018 another law reversed Evo Morales' longstanding opposition to biofuels (biodiesel from soy and ethanol from sugar). Confronting a fuel shortage and intense pressure from the soy and sugar industry, the government moved to promote plant-based fuel production and promised to buy ethanol. This incentivized more deforestation. In April of 2019, just a few months before his ouster, Morales signed the decree to facilitate approval of two new GMO soy varieties resistant to both drought and glyphosate. The reason was that the soy frontier was expanding into the dry forest area of the Chiquitanía region, and farmers hoped it would do better there. At the same time, the government passed a law that in effect reduced sanctions and fines on burning, implicitly encouraging new fires. In June of 2019 a presidential decree authorized new deforestation in areas of Santa Cruz and Beni departments (Villalobos 2020; Gustafson 2020b). The combined interest in expanding soy and sugar frontiers for biofuels and expanding cattle production for exports to China both implicated government policy as a proximate incentive for burning (CEDIB 2020). Even if he did not light the match, Evo's policies certainly helped shape conditions for the inferno.

Environmentalist NGOs have worked to draw attention to these contradictions of the MAS government in relation to the Amazon basin. Yet the question of the fires, the Amazon, and the environment have also entered a polarized political sphere. Paradoxically, right-leaning political actors and urbanites have held up the issue of the "environment" as a way to attack Evo Morales, as early as 2011, during the

TIPNIS conflicts.[3] At that time, a plan to build a highway through a protected area and Indigenous territory led to intense conflicts between Indigenous organizations the government. Although many on the left, including those formerly sympathetic to the MAS were also critical, what was surprising was the way that otherwise reactionary actors also transformed, virtually overnight, into defenders of nature and of Indigenous rights. This pattern continued in subsequent years, as organizations like *Ríos de Pie* (Standing Rivers) emerged as outlets for environmental attacks on Evo Morales, even though their funders and supporters were aligned with right-leaning 'human rights' organizations. Leading up to the November 2019 coup, with the fires burning, these organizations once again organized social media campaigns like #SOSBolivia, which seemed to suggest that Evo Morales was solely to blame for the devastation. Curiously, and unaware of Bolivia's internal politics, even European organizations like #ExtinctionRebellion amplified these campaigns, which were more aimed at destroying the reputation of Evo Morales than in promoting progressive environmental policies. During the year of right-wing control that followed the coup, with the fires burning once again and new decrees emitted to support agro-industrial expansion, these same organizations were largely silent. The challenge going forward will be to align the goals and projects of wider social movements with a new vision of agro-ecological change, rather than supporting the co-optation of environmentalist discourse and the cynical exploitation of Indigenous peoples by conservative political groups.

The coup regime

When Evo left the country in 2019, a government led by Jeanine Áñez took control. Áñez was part of the "Demócratas" party, a political vehicle with its base among the agrarian elite of eastern Bolivia. She was allied with a more extreme sector of that elite as well, the forces tied to Luís Fernando Camacho and his soy and vegetable oil baron backer, Branko Marinkovic. Marinkovic had been living in exile since 2009, having been accused of participating in a plot to kill Evo Morales. Yet after the coup, he came back. His family is one of the largest landowners in the east. Like many, his family has used the state (especially subsidized loans and low taxes) to accumulate wealth, and unsurprisingly has sent earnings overseas for sheltering, as revealed in the Panama Papers. Between the Demócratas and this more reactionary political sector, it was clear that coup government represented the agro-industrial elite. By the end of Áñez' time in office, Marinkovic himself was named Minister of Development and Planning, a far cry from his alleged role in a criminal plot from years before.

The interim government made a number of policy moves that sought to take advantage of presidential decree power. In relation to land policy, the new president handed over control of the national land reform office (INRA) to the wealthy, naming Eliane Capobianco, also a representative of the eastern agrarian elite, as Minister of Rural Development and Lands. Capobianco, to Indigenous movements and environmentalists alike, was a notorious figure. In the early days of the MAS, when the country was rewriting the constitution, she is remembered for her racist statements in the constitutional assembly, admonishing Quechua representatives to either speak Spanish or remain silent (Gustafson 2009a). Capobianco had been a director of INRA in the pre-Morales era, during which time she was accused of running a network of corruption that used the agency to benefit large landowners. Her own family was involved in fraudulent efforts to avoid the payment of taxes. The family of Branko Marinkovic was also implicated in these corruption rings (*La Prensa* 2007). She was also an advisor to the cattlemen's chamber of Santa Cruz (FEGASACRUZ) and the Association of Vegetable Oil Producers (ANAPO), both entities tied to the most conservative factions of the agrarian capitalist elite. In this context, the government set about signing an accord with the agrarian chamber of commerce (CAO) that actually directed the land reform office to confirm thousands of acres of land titles for businesses.

In May of 2020, the President of Bolivia, Jeanine Áñez, signed into law a Supreme Decree (DS 4348), that allowed for the identification of areas for the use of GMO corn. Over 100 social organizations and NGOs immediately cried foul, signing a manifesto that decried the move, arguing that not only would it incentivize further deforestation (and fires, already raging at the time), it was an attack on the "genetic patrimony" of the country (Página Siete 2020). Just a few months earlier the Áñez government had also signed another decree (DS 4232) that removed obstacles to the approval of GMO corn, sugar, cotton, wheat, and soy – abbreviating oversight processes that are established in the Constitution. Although GMO corn has been planted illegally since at least 2015, the agro-industrial elite wanted to legalize and expand its use as it had done with soy, along with these other crops (Fundación Tierra 2020:24). Furthermore, the government of Áñez itself was seen by many as illegitimate – or at least as lacking a mandate – having come to power after the social upheaval and the forced resignation of Evo Morales in November of 2019. It seemed that the so-called "interim government" which represented by proxy and in the flesh the agro-industrial elite of eastern Bolivia, was working as fast as it could to deepen the political grip that these agrarian elites have long held over land policy in Bolivia.

In May of 2020, as the interim President signed the pro-GMO decree, the agribusiness chamber (CAO, Cámara Agropecuaria del Oriente) also staged a press conference to tout a supposed agreement with a lowland Indigenous organization, the Confederación Indígena del Oriente Boliviano (CIDOB). Though it did not mention GMO seeds specifically, the stunt was aimed at performing a convergence of interests between Indigenous organizations and big agro-capital. Other Indigenous organizations denounced the agreement as a farce, and the CIDOB itself denied that the individuals signing the document had any authority. But in point of fact, in early 2019 a more curious statement emerged from the peasant unions of the northern Santa Cruz region. Though ostensibly identified with the MAS, the organization issued a statement supporting the expansion of GMOs, suggesting efforts by big business to cajole – or coerce – smaller growers into supporting GMO seeds. As with other policies tied to land and territory, this revealed a schism between those more commercially oriented farmers and Indigenous organizations (CIPCA 2019). The bigger point is clear: the agro-industrial elite are determined to use deceptive and illegitimate strategies to defend their interests. In addition, the event brought to light a deeper problem inherited from the MAS period: the division of Indigenous movements and the coopting of leaders separated from the organic decision-making control of their bases.

Futures of policy and movement

The country went to the polls for the second time in a year in October of 2020, and handed the reins of government back to the MAS party with an overwhelming vote of 55% going to candidate Luís Arce. While political tensions remain high, particularly with the arch-conservative – fascist to many – sectors of Santa Cruz, Arce appears to have a mandate for a five-year term. Whether this new era will reflect a continuity of the more conciliatory relationship to agrarian capital remains unclear. Arce, who was Evo Morales' Minister of the Economy for most of his 14 years in office, is known to be a backer of the biofuel idea. Yet the rising tensions with the most conservative sectors of the agrarian elite might lead Arce to return to a more assertive stance, calling on the social movements to support his government and its policies. At this writing, predictions are difficult.

What is clear is that the often-repeated critique of extractivism (whether of gas, soy, or minerals) is generally unable to mobilize alternative visions of agricultural production in eastern Bolivia. The seemingly unassailable hegemony of the soy and cattle industries has been critiqued through two lenses – that of GMOs and that of deforestation and fires. These are useful mobilizing points but do not alone offer political visions of alternative land use. The underlying assumption appears to be that smaller-scale agriculture, some form of organic or alternative projects, and more diverse forms of land use would be good. Yet the precondition for such projects would be the state's withdrawal of subsidies to big agriculture and state's commitment to effective redistribution. These would both entail dismantling a hegemonic bloc, and perhaps, state or popular violence, both of which seem unlikely. What might unravel in the longer term could be a destruction of the soy market through expansion of electric vehicles (thus collapsing demand for biofuels) and the resurgence of more militant peasant organizations in the face of urban poverty and lack of employment (similar to the MST in Brazil, whose short-lived Bolivian counterpart was demobilized by the Morales government). More research and creative thinking are needed to document the situation of rural Bolivia – both in the high Andes and in the agrarian landscapes of the east. Bolivian NGOs and social movements may find new synergies in the new political moment, but it remains to be seen if the new MAS government will continue to back the subordination to global agro-capital or whether the government can use its power to help create a new agrarian model. As this went to press and the country prepared to inaugurate Luís Arce as the new president of Bolivia, Bayer Bolivia (the new name of the company formed from the merger of Bayer and Monsanto) was touting its promotion of a contest that a Bolivian NGO was participating in. The winner would receive a cash prize, and would promote "new seeds for the future". While the shape and terms of land struggle, reform, and revolution have shifted in new ways, and amid new complexities, the struggle in defense of nature, human well-being, and for a more egalitarian society and distribution of the means of production is still being waged against the interests of multinational capital.

Notes

1 For comparison, Argentina has been mostly urban since the 1950s, and is currently 92% urban (CEPA 2019).

2 As documented by Lastarria-Cornhiel (2009:225–26), it was not until mid-2003 that INRA directors issued memoranda requiring the participation of women in meetings. The neoliberal project began to unravel with the Gas War of October 2003 (Gustafson 2020a).

3 The TIPNIS conflicts stemmed from government efforts to build a highway through a protected Indigenous area (the "Territorio Indígena y Parque Nacional Isiboro-Sécure", hence TIPNIS). See McNeish (2013).

References

https://www.beyondpesticides.org/assets/media/documents/Glufosinate ChemWatch.pdf

CEDIB (2020) *Los incendios en la Chiquitanía el 2019: políticas devastadoras, acciones irresponsables y negligencia gubernamental.* CEDIB, La Paz. https://cedib.org/wp-content/uploads/2020/09/Dossier-Incendios-Chiquitania.pdf. Accessed October 29, 2020.

CEPA (2019) 'Latin America and the Caribbean: Population Estimates and Projections.' *Economic Commission for Latin America and the Caribbean.* https://www.cepal.org/en/topics/demographic-projections/latin-america-and-caribbean-population-estimates-and-projections. Accessed November 4, 2020.

CIPCA (2019). 'La Confederación de Pueblos Indígenas de Bolivia rechaza la liberación de semillas transgénicas', 31 January. https://cipca.org.bo/noticias/la-confederacion-de-pueblos-indigenas-de-bolivia-rechaza-la-liberacion-de-semillas-transgenicas

Colque, G. (2020) 'Los patrones del oriente y los transgénicos.' Fundación Tierra, La Paz. 1 September. https://ftierra.org/index.php/opinion-y-analisis/957-los-patrones-del-oriente-y-los-transgenicos. Accessed November 3, 2020.

Colque, G., Tinta, E. and Sanjinés, E. (2016) *Segunda reforma agraria: una historia que incomoda.* Fundación Tierra, La Paz.

Deere, C. D. and León, M. (2001) *Empowering Women: Land and Property Rights in Latin America.* University of Pittsburgh Press, Pittsburgh.

Farthing, L. and Kohl, B. (2006) *Impasse in Bolivia: Neoliberal Hegemony and Popular Resistance.* Zed, London.

Fundación Tierra (2020) *¿Qué hay detrás de los transgénicos?: Tenencia de la tierra, agronegocio y rendimientos.* Foro Virtual, June. Fundación Tierra, La Paz. https://ftierra.org/index.php?option=com_mtree&task=att_download&link_id=197&cf_id=52. Accessed October 27, 2020.

Garcés, F. (2011) 'The Domestication of Indigenous Autonomies in Bolivia: From the Pact of Unity to the New Constitution.' In Fabricant, N. and Gustafson B. (eds) *Remapping Bolivia.* SAR Press, Santa Fe.

Gustafson, B. (2006) 'Spectacles of Autonomy and Crisis: Or, What Bulls and Beauty Queens Have to Do with Regionalism in Eastern Bolivia.' *Journal of Latin American and Caribbean Anthropology*, vol 11, no 2, pp351–379.

Gustafson, B. (2009a). *New Languages of the State: Indigenous Resurgence and the Politics of Knowledge in Bolivia.* Duke University Press, Durham.

Gustafson, B (2009b) 'Manipulating Cartographies: Plurinationalism, Autonomy, and Indigenous Resurgence in Bolivia.' *Anthropological Quarterly*, vol 82, no 4, pp985–1016.

Gustafson, B (2020a). *Bolivia in the Age of Gas.* Duke University Press, Durham.

Gustafson, B. (2020b). 'Bolivia's Amazon: Power and Politics Fanning the Flames.' *ReVista: Harvard Review of Latin America* (April 2020). https://

revista.drclas.harvard.edu/book/bolivia%E2%80%99s-amazon. Accessed November 1, 2020.

IARC (International Agency for Research on Cancer) (2016) 'Q&A on Glyphosate' Lyon (France): World Health Organization. https://www.iarc.fr/wp-content/uploads/2018/11/QA_Glyphosate.pdf. Accessed November 4, 2020.

Inturias, M., Vargas, M., Rodríguez, I, García, A., von Stosch, K. and Masay, E. (eds) (2018) *Territorios, justicias, autonomías: un diálogo desde los gobiernos autónomos indígenas de Bolivia.* Editorial Nur, Santa Cruz.

La Prensa (2007) 'Branco Marinkovic dice que es inocente y que se defenderá en la justicia.' June 29.

Lastarria-Cornhiel, S. (2009) 'Land Tenure, Titling, and Gender in Bolivia.' *St. Louis University Public Law Review*, vol 29, no 1, pp193–242.

Mamani, M. I. (2020a) 'La lucha por la tierra no ha terminado: situación de las mujeres campesinas en Bolivia.' *Fundación Tierra Serie Informes/País.* June 2020. Fundación Tierra, La Paz. https://ftierra.org/index.php?option=com_mtree&task=att_download&link_id=194&cf_id=52. Accessed October 27, 2020.

Mamani, M. I. (2020b) 'La copropiedad de la tierra es insuficiente para la equidad de género.' *Fundación Tierra.* July 31. https://ftierra.org/index.php/opinion-y-analisis/952-la-copropiedad-de-la-tierra-es-insuficiente-para-la-equidad-de-genero. Accessed October 30, 2020.

McKay, B. (2018) *Extractivismo agrario: dinámicas de poder, acumulación y exclusión en Bolivia.* Fundación Tierra, La Paz.

McKay, B. and Colque, G. (2016) 'Bolivia's Soy Complex: The Development of 'Productive Exclusion.' *The Journal of Peasant Studies*, vol 43, no 2, pp583–610.

McNeish, J. A. (2013) 'Extraction, Protest, and Indigeneity in Bolivia: The TIPNIS Effect.' *Latin American and Caribbean Ethnic Studies*, vol 8, no 2, pp221–242.

Molina, P. (2020) 'Transgénicos de cuarentena.' *Fundación Agrecol Andes.* https://www.agrecolandes.org/2020/05/14/transgenicos-de-cuarentena/. Accessed October 30, 2020.

Morell i Torra, P. (2018) '"Pronto aquí vamos a mandar nosotros": Autonomía Guarani Charagua Iyambae, la construcción de un proyecto político indígena en la Bolivia plurinacional.' PhD diss., Universitat de Barcelona.

Página Siete (2020) 'Organizaciones: DS 4348 desconoce que Bolivia es centro de origen de maíz.' 25 September. https://www.paginasiete.bo/economia/2020/9/25/organizaciones-ds-4348-desconoce-que-bolivia-es-centro-de-origen-del-maiz-269365.html

Tockman, J. (2017) 'La construcción de Autonomía Indígena en Bolivia.' Fundación Tierra, La Paz. http://www.ftierra.org/index.php/opinion-y-analisis/747-la-construccion-de-autonomia-indigena-en-bolivia. Accessed October 28, 2020.

Villalobos, G. (2020) 'Las leyes incendiarias en Bolivia.' *Fundación Solón.* https://fundacionsolon.org/2020/02/20/las-leyes-incendiarias-en-wwbolivia/#_ftn4. Accessed October 29, 2020.

5 Lithium and *vivir bien*

Sovereignty and transition

Fabio S. M. Castro, Sinclair M. G. Guerra and Paulo A. Lima Filho

Introduction

At the entrance of the new century, a proposal for a sovereign nation project based on the emancipation of indigenous and peasant communities emerged in Bolivia. Under the indigenous leadership of Evo Morales, through the social movements organization, it took advantage of the commodity boom and distributed income in the country, a process that came to be known as 'Bolivian Wonder'. It was a process that started in 2006 and that lasted for almost 14 years. Although interrupted for one year by a military coup, the path to *vivir bien* (living well), even if plunged into deep contradictions, is expected to resume after the democratic elections at the end of 2020.

This historical process, which is known in the country as *proceso de cambio* (process of change), even after the crisis in 2009 and the sharp drop in commodity prices in 2014, which led other South American countries into deep crises, permitted a continued growth at around 5% per year. However, this did not prevent a reaction of the traditional elites against this popular project. Riding the wave of the strengthening of the extreme right in the region, at the end of 2019, against the result of the elections that would lead to a fourth term of the Movement toward Socialism (*Movimiento al Socialismo* – MAS), the Bolivian middle class took to the streets expressing their discontent and, supported by the military, they pressured Evo Morales to resign.

We interpret what happened as a coup d'état, as do Lambert (2019) and Engdahl (2019). At the international level, discussions about whether it was a coup or not were intense. The hegemonic media attested to the legitimacy of the facts in view of their origin in the manifestations of the middle class; nonetheless, they failed to consider the external influence that was established and the definitive participation of the military who were co-opted to reinforce the coup.

On the other side, in alternative media outlets, a narrative that indicated the link between the coup and the interests of North American companies in the Bolivian lithium was consolidated. This narrative got even stronger when Elon Musk – CEO of Tesla, one of the largest producers of electric cars in the world – published on his Twitter account, in response to a provocation regarding North American interventionism in Bolivia: 'We will coup whoever we want. Deal with it'.[1] To many, this confirmed that the Bolivian coup was motivated by an interest to gain access to the country's large reserves of lithium, a mineral used for the manufacturing of electric batteries. Evidently, Musk made a very serious statement. But to really apprehend the role of lithium it is necessary to understand that Bolivia sought to insert itself sovereignly in the world lithium market, breaking with its traditional position in the international division of labor.

This historical construction of capitalism tells us that the system is governed by uneven development that keeps countries that are already developed rich, and the underdeveloped countries poor (Fernandes 1976). A structural system opposition between center and periphery is called imperialism from the perspective of Amin (2015). According to this author (2014, 2015), we live in an era of generalized monopolies, in which transnational companies control the dynamic of the system. However, power is determined by the dominant states in a kind of collective imperialism. For the author, globalization only exists due to the interventions of US armed forces, and the administration of the dollar as a system is managed by state instruments, not the market. Thus, collective imperialism acts offensively in the world, in two ways. In the economic sphere, it imposes globalized neoliberalism and in the political sphere, it promotes a system of continuous intervention, through the five monopolies: technological, financial, natural resources, communications, and military (Amin 2003).

In other words, imperialist states, through their large transnational companies, in oligopolistic markets that have technological supremacy, establish themselves globally through the financial market, demanding the internal deregulation of dominated countries and cheap access to natural resources and the workforce. To ensure that this system works, there is constant ideological control through the media and the maintenance of submissive armed forces, whether ideologically or under pressure from the power of arms. This makes the possibility of development in the global south unfeasible. Capitalism manages to maintain its accumulation along the same lines as the colonial system: ultra-exploitation of labor, deepened by the technological increase in productivity and by, often masked, structural racism that keeps societies segregated; plus the plundering of the land, expressed in natural resources extractivism. (Harvey 2003; Nascimento 2016; Veltmeyer and Petras 2019). A neocolonial system disguised as globalization.

The rise of Morales is directly marked by an anti-imperialist character. His plan to develop Bolivia had as a starting point national sovereignty, and in this, the Bolivian lithium industrialization strategy is a central element. The country has the world's largest reserves of this metal, which in recent decades has become central to the geopolitics of energy. In this sense, the goal of this chapter is to demystify the economic project of the 'process of change' and situate the lithium industrialization strategy in the context of Bolivia's extractivist economic model. Furthermore, the chapter seeks to assess the role of lithium in one of the main challenges to be faced by the MAS's fourth term, i.e. the return to the path of prosperity and income distribution, after the economic paralysis caused by the coup d'état and the health crisis of the Covid-19 pandemic.

In the first part, we discuss the new economic model developed during the Morales government to overcome underdevelopment in Bolivia and its intrinsic relationship with *vivir bien*. In the second part, we discuss the importance and potential of lithium for the Bolivian resource industrialization strategy and in the third part we discuss the present geopolitical context and its implications. The three discussions combined lead to the conclusion that in Bolivia there is a continual political process that is intrinsically linked to social movements organization and economically based on extractivism, while its direction is guided by a permanent change to a post-capitalist perspective.

The Bolivian Wonder

Bolivia has historically been subjected to a social apartheid regime that has kept wealth in the hands of white and creole elites, while a multitude of indigenous people and their descendants have been embittered by poverty and social and political exclusion. The country has enormous mineral and hydrocarbon reserves that underlay the centuries-long natural resource exploitation, since colonial times. Today Bolivia is the country with the lowest per capita income in the region,[2] where the colonial heritage still marks its socioeconomic situation.

The rise of a popular leader into the ranks of government in Bolivia is the result of a long historical process. The resistance to neoliberalism exploded in the paradigmatic Water War in 2000 and became effective with the 2005 election of Evo Morales as the country's first indigenous president, who promised fundamental transformations to construct a fairer and more egalitarian society. The Andean indigenous worldview laid at the base of this political project through the preponderant role of (indigenous) social movements. Amin (1989) proposes the idea that America is historically transmuted to be an extension of Europe, where the hegemony of social construction is guided by Eurocentrism. However, in Bolivia, society remained divided or *abigarrada,* therefore, other worldviews have prevailed next to ethnic apartheid (Zavaleta Mercado 1990). The rise of the MAS promotes precisely the political emancipation of the indigenous worldviews, mainly originating from the peasants and Andean indigenous people, that enters in conflict with Eurocentrism, in an intercultural perspective (Albó 2008).

The above has resulted in a dialectical process marked by the struggle to build a decolonized state while resisting neoliberalism, distribute income without dismantling traditional elites, preserve the environment while maintaining the economy's extractive activities, build national sovereignty amid structural dependency, move towards socialism without breaking with great private property. These are some of the contradictions that emerge in the national project proposed to Bolivia with the rise of MAS to power, expressed in the two fundaments of this process: the new economic model and the *vivir bien*.

New economic model

Bolivia's new economic model was presented as an antithesis of the neoliberal model and with a view to transition to a new society. In other words, it is a 'transitional project' whose horizon is the so-called community socialism to 'living well'. For Farah H. and Vasapollo (2016), this horizon has its origins in the recovery of debates that question the individualistic and economicist unilateralism of the capitalist rationality, which in its neoliberal phase is increasingly unfair, depredating, and undemocratic.

In this perspective, the new model is based on three areas: *Social*, to solve social problems before individual ones; *Community*, for privileging the common before the individual, and for being aligned with native peoples' traditions and values; and *Productive*, to transform the productive model and overcome poverty in a dignified, sustainable and responsible way. Hence the name: *New Social, Community, and Productive Economic Model* (Arce Catacora 2011). The goal is to free Bolivia from the primary-exporter model to build an economy based on industry and high productivity. Nevertheless, as a transitional model, it means that Bolivia will remain a supplier of raw materials, at least in the short and medium-term. The change is that, with the nationalization of natural resources, the surpluses of extractivism are distributed to transform the country.

The new economic model is established in two pillar sectors. The *Strategic Sector* based on natural resources is responsible for generating economic surpluses and is managed by strategic public companies;

the *Employment and Income Generating Sector* brings together private companies, cooperatives, and communities to transform the country's production structure (Arce Catacora 2011).

In short, the model is based on the distribution of economic surpluses generated in the *strategic sector* through the role of the State. The proposed transition aims to overcome, in the first place, the poor distribution of income in the country and diversify the economy, so that, in the long run, conditions are made possible for a society that transcends capitalism. For this, the new economic model is based on a pragmatic macroeconomic policy that uses Keynesian concepts to organize the country and maintain stability.[3]

With a stable economy, the *Employment and Income Generating Sector* finances investment, primarily through the Bank of Productive Development (BDP). In addition, there are subsidies and incentives for the industrialization of manufacturing, tourism, agricultural development, transportation, handicrafts, housing, and commerce. This allows the Bolivian currency to circulate more intensively internally in the country, strengthening economic relations, avoiding dollarization, and controlling inflation. Figure 5.1 shows the flowchart of the model.

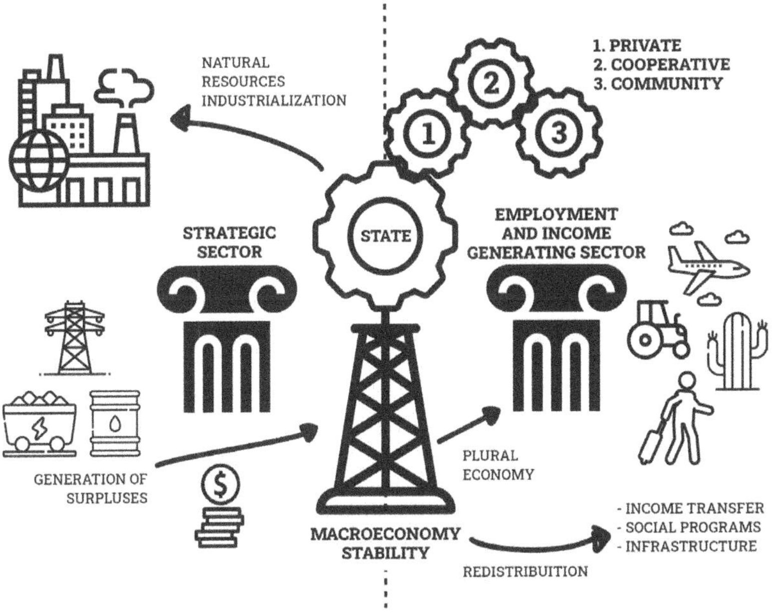

Figure 5.1 Flowchart of the New Social, Community and Productive Economic Model.

Source: own elaboration, adapted from Arce Catacora (2011).

The new economic model is based both on the exploitation of natural resources and on a pragmatic macroeconomic policy, while deployed through public investment and income distribution. Natural resources were nationalized in 2006, through Supreme Decree (DS) No. 28701, envisioning a model marked by the exploitation of resources through joint ventures with foreign companies. In this process, contracts with multinationals were reviewed and adapted to the guidelines of the new policy.[4] The process also relied on some advantageous developments in the international market, particularly the rise in the price of commodities. Roca Sanchéz (2017: 23) indicates that gas income jumped from an annual average of US$ 888 million between 2000 and 2005 to US$ 4,316 million between 2006 and 2015. In combination with the nationalization of the hydrocarbon sector, this explains the growth of gas exports volume by 69%, between 2005 and 2014, and an increase of the gas income by more than 450% in the same period (INE 2020). In Bolivia, as well as in other countries in the region, the increasing global demand stimulated the economy's concentration on commodities. The positive results lead to consistent economic growth and enabled a great leap in the country's income distribution. Despite some significant progress, the economic structure has remained largely unchanged. Looking at the Bolivian export agenda, there is a noticeable concentration on a few economic activities. In 2013, gas alone accounted for almost 50% of Bolivian exports (INE). The first two terms of Morales (2006–2014) were marked by this high liquidity from exports, on average around 43% of GDP.

The economic policy of the Morales administration has shown to be conscious of the risks involved in maintaining an economic model based on commodity export, and has proposed to overcome it by a two-fold strategy: the diversification of the primary export matrix and the industrialization of natural resources. The diversification of the export matrix answers to the realization that the good yields from the gas export would not last much longer. Brazil, the largest importer of Bolivian gas, has shown an inclination to become self-reliant in the medium term, through the pre-salt resources.[5] This has stimulated the strategy to find an alternative to gas while transforming Bolivia into an 'energetic power' (ENDE 2018). Today, approximately 64% of the energy generated in Bolivia is through thermoelectric plants using gas. Still, there is a great impetus to move to renewable sources, including wind, solar, and biomass projects which already generate 6% of the country's energy.

Yet the core of the strategy is found in the further development of hydroelectric plants – currently producing 30%. The aim is to generate up to 74% renewable energy, with a capacity to export 12,000 MW (Castro and Rosental 2017). A project like this is viable, but it is not without impediments. On the one hand, it takes time to consolidate as it depends on the construction of joint transmission infrastructure between the countries involved. On the other hand, the construction of large hydroelectric power plants has a major local impact on the environment and social organization. This has triggered environmental and social conflicts that have slowed down the implementation of projects, and have made clear that it is necessary to mitigate and compensate for social and environmental damage.

Another area of export diversification lies in the agribusiness, with the expansion of the agricultural frontier. Between 2005 and 2019, agriculture jumped from 2.4 million to 3.8 million hectares, marking a 59% expansion on the agricultural frontier (INE). In this regard, products derived from soy have significant values, with export volumes jumping from 1.3 million tons in 2005 to 2 million tons in 2019. At its peak in 2014, the export value of soy products reached almost a billion dollars.

All of this data indicates that the Bolivian economy has remained anchored in the logic of the export primary products, where the six most relevant products from the list of Bolivian exportables (gas, fuels, zinc, silver, gold, and soybeans) accounted for approximately 70% in 2018. The most important industrialization projects to break with this are that of gas and lithium, which have received the highest volumes of investment in the country's history.[6] It must be emphasized that the industrialization projects are at an initial stage, heavily dependent on continuous investment while facing impediments related to infrastructure, education, and knowledge and technology.

The second part of the new economic plan refers to pragmatic macroeconomic policy. According to Luis Arce Catacora (2011), stability is not an end on its own, as in the neoliberal logic, but the starting point to structural economic transformation. This translates into a rather contradictory situation in which the state's sovereignty is reasserted in macroeconomic policies while seeking to maintain alignment with the international market.

At the national level, the goal is to pursue social inclusion through employment and income, to stimulate domestic demand, to reduce external dependence, and to maintain price and currency stability:

an endogenous development project. In parallel, there is the accumulation of international reserves from the *strategic sector* surplus, increasing from US$ 1,795 billion in 2005 to US$ 1,513 billion in 2014, accounting for approximately 45% of GDP in the same year.

Bolivia's macroeconomic policies under the MAS administration have garnered praise from the IMF (2018), in consideration of the positive results achieved: average economic growth of 5% per year; average controlled inflation of 5.2%; unemployment below 4% since 2008; exchange Rate (USD/BOL) controlled by 6.91 since 2012 (World Bank indicators 2020). In the first two terms of Morales, given the international liquidity and the nationalizations, it was possible to build this economic stability, while keeping the tensions around the development project relatively controlled. By the end of 2014 commodity prices begin to plummet on the international market, submerging almost all countries of the region in economic crisis, affecting particularly the exporter sector. The weight of exports to Bolivia's economy fell from 43% of GDP in 2014 to 31% in 2015 and 24% in 2016. Still, the economy remained growing, contrary to what happened in other countries in the region, mainly due to the countercyclical policy measures during Morales' third term.

Reserves at the end of 2018 were US$ 8,929 billion, equivalent to GDP of 22%. The adoption of a more accelerated endogenous growth strategy to supply the drop in the share of exports in the country's GDP managed to maintain economic growth. But it came at a political cost: growing contradictions around power at the domestic level. The eastern provinces, particularly Santa Cruz, receive the largest volume of income from the country's exportable products. The abrupt fall in export results destabilized the political balance that had been attained by means of concessions for the approval of the 2009 Constitution, reigniting regional polarization.

Income distribution was able to relieve more than 3 million people from poverty, contributing to a development by which Bolivia became the country with the best indicators of inequality reduction of the region in the period 2006–2018, according to the Gini index (Table 5.1). The two impulses of this process were the conditional cash transfer programs – the so-called *bonos* – and the increase in the minimum wage, which jumped almost 500% in nominal terms (INE). Table 5.1 presents some selected social indicators that illustrate these advances.

Amidst the promotion of industrialization, the diversification of production, building infrastructure and social spending, public investment rose sharply from US$ 629 million in 2005 to US$ 5,323 by 2019.

This process provided the impetus to transform the domestic market into one of the main growth drivers in the country. The resources used for this almost 750% expansion in investment originated from surpluses of the *strategic sector*, in the first two terms of Morales, and from indebtedness and use of reserves in the third. Morales took over the country with an external debt/GDP ratio of 52% (2005), achieving in 2014 an index of 18%. With the crisis starting at the end of 2014, this logic changed, raising indebtedness at the same time that part of the reserves were used to maintain the public investment, as can be seen in Figure 5.2. This external balance made it possible for Bolivia to adopt

Table 5.1 Social indicators advancement in the 'process of change'

Indicator\Year	*2005*	*2018*
Extreme poverty (% population)	16.4%	4.1%
Poverty (% população)	59.6%	34.6%
Inequality (GINI index)	58.5	42.2
Participation in income of the richest 10%	45.3%	30.4%
Participation in income of the poorest 20%	2%	4.6%
Minimum wage (in current USD)	US$63.68	US$307.09[2019]
Access to electricity (% population)	68.28%	95.58%
Access to basic sanitation (% population)	43.5% [2001]	57.1%[2015]

Source: World Bank (2020), INE (2020), MMAyA (2017).

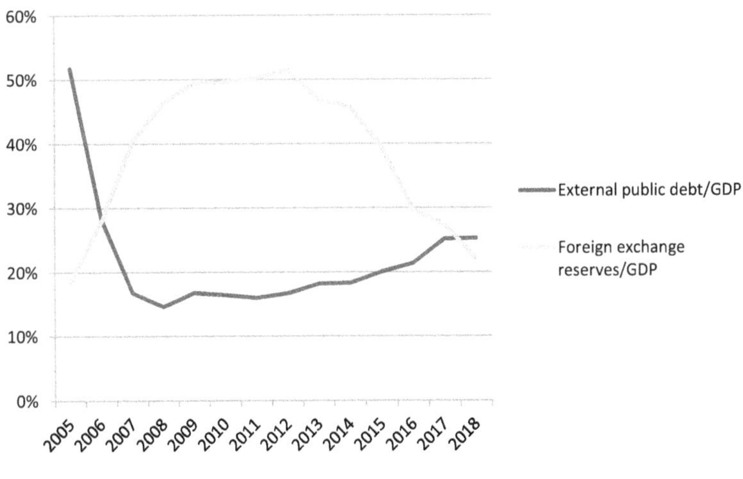

Figure 5.2 Ratio (%) of GDP with external public debt and foreign exchange reserves.

Source: own elaboration from BCB (2020).

autonomous policies, without resorting to the IMF for example, even in crisis, through anti-cyclical policy.

Next to productive investments and social spending, an effort has been made to update the archaic infrastructural situation of the country. Infrastructural investment constituted a boost to the country's integration, whether through paving highways, urban transport, access to electricity, or telecommunications.

In short, this is the model proposed to overcome underdevelopment, achieve national sovereignty, reduce inequalities, and eradicate poverty. For authors like Katz (2015), Gudynas (2011), Postero (2017), it is a social developmental model that has encountered difficulties to achieve the structural transformation and that is still far from the ideal of 'living well'. According to these authors, much of the success of the 'process of change' is due to the fact that the Bolivian starting point was so backward that there was much room for great initial qualitative leaps.

Transitioning to vivir bien

The ideal of *vivir bien* constitutes the horizon of the transitional economic model. *Vivir bien* has been characterized as a collective construction, a non-monolithic process, and a utopia. For this reason, it engenders great and controversial debates in scientific and political discussions around the world (Ranta 2016).

In the Bolivian Constitution (Bolivia 2009: 158), *vivir bien* is placed as the supreme objective of the Plurinational State. The former president (Morales Ayma 2011) sees *vivir bien* as a system that transcends capitalism, a doctrine and practice that is based on the philosophy of Indigenous Peoples. He points out the need to build a society for 'living well', based on ethical and moral principles that stand as the antithesis of capitalism, and put forward 'community socialism' as its way of consolidating it. He emphasizes that it can only be built on the basis of life in harmony with nature and complementarity between peoples.

Farah H. and Vasapollo (2016) interpret the Bolivian attempts to implement 'living well' as a renewal of humanism and environmentalism, that intersects with the re-emergence of the peasant and indigenous movement against the crushing of workers by neoliberalism. In this sense, the authors argue that these claims go beyond the discussion about the emancipation of the working class, as they are based on the recognition and recovery of their own social reproduction experiences.

Thus, the ideal of 'living well' leads us to understand that it is fundamentally an ethical principle that shapes discourses and seeks a balance with practice to advance the transition to a new society.

The political interpretation of 'living well' has been subject to much criticism for the permanent contradiction between pursuing the *vivir bien* and using the resources of extractivism for its realization. Gudynas (2011) complains that the Plurinational Constitution does not recognize the rights of nature. For Stefanoni (2012), policies could not and did not try to reflect the worldview of the native communities. Lalander (2016), points to an extractive dilemma, where the rights of nature and the indigenous people suffer a partial and selective sacrifice to supposedly achieve the objectives of general social welfare. The author indicates the reinforced ethnic character of the Morales government at the global level, while often relativized in favor of extractivism at the local.

For Linera (2019), the nationalization of natural resources cannot be fully achieved without an industrialization stage. It is necessary to offer goods with added value in global value chains to boost income and to promote greater productivity in Bolivia, along with technological management and scientific knowledge. Nevertheless, the author understands that this process generates undesired results regarding the environment, even if the end is the satisfaction of human needs, not profit. In his words 'damages that, in the long run, irrevocably affect the human being … We have to avoid this fatal destiny' (ibid.: 64).

Linera situates the solution in the community's productive forces, starting from the conception that 'the community' proposes a different form of social development in which nature is conceived as an organic extension of human subjectivity. However, he reinforces the idea that industrialization and science, which can generate material and technological conditions for production that is more adequate to human and natural needs, is necessary to transfer power to workers (ibid.).

On this point Stefanoni (2012) disagrees. In his view, the economic pluralism model that projects a final solution in communities does not give due importance to workers, touching upon the key point of this transition which is still poorly resolved in the Bolivian model. The way to systematically transfer the political and productive power from the state level to the community level of the associated workers remains to be elucidated.

Linera (2018: 118) believes that 'the State cannot create the community, because it is the perfect antithesis of the community … The State itself is unable to restore the life-giving metabolism between human beings and nature'. In this sense, a State within the scope of the 'transition' has the purpose of protecting the anti-capitalist community and cooperative initiatives and improve the living conditions of workers. In that way, the workers are given time to try new social forms until it is possible to overcome the bourgeois order in a universal and irreversible movement.

In our view, *vivir bien* as a more ideological measure can be thought of as the cultural revolution necessary to move toward a society that transcends capitalism. Something like the 'new man' thought by Ernesto 'Ché' Guevara (Löwy 2003) that overcomes the limitations of 20th-century socialism and moves toward a break with a mercantile and destructive society, to find balance between human life and nature. Therefore, the historical and transforming meaning of *vivir bien* refers to the search for the construction of balance in a plurinational society. This process takes place in a context full of imperfections arising from five centuries of institutional violence, and despite its intrinsic contradictions, it has managed to achieve significant economic and social emancipatory improvements. However, in addition to a sovereign nation project and the solution of some historical problems, new tensions and contradictions have emerged. That is why the possibility of looking at an emancipated horizon for the Bolivian people is only real to the extent that a long process of decolonization and the construction of a new society is assumed. The aim to develop the lithium industry can be seen as emblematic of the intrinsic contradictions of the 'process of change'. Despite being inserted in a still extractivist perspective, this is the main Bolivian bet to generate material conditions to overcome underdevelopment through the transition project.

Reasserting sovereignty in the Bolivian lithium project

Given its strategic character for the current global energy transition and the fact that Bolivia has the largest reserve in the world, the lithium strategy was configured as the main bet of MAS to overcome underdevelopment in the country.

Lithium is the lightest of the components in the metal chain and has great electrochemical and energetic potential, which gives it 'exclusive properties to store and transport significant electrical charges' (Gouze 2010: 84). Therefore, portable devices that need autonomy of displacement, such as smartphones, computers, tablets, cameras, drones, electric cars etc., use lithium batteries. The emergence of new battery technologies, in the 2010s, promoted the initial dissemination of the so-called Electric Vehicles (EV) (Narins 2017) as the starting point for solving the problem of fossil fuels, as the capacity to store allows the use of alternative sources of energy generation.[7] Although EVs is not likely to solve the energy generation problem, it is significant in as much as it breaks the exclusivity of fossil fuels. In other words, EVs facilitate the decarbonization of the system and, therefore, are central to the global energy transition.

On the other hand, it is important to highlight that lithium extraction has a process with a strong impact on the environment. Takemura (2018) indicates that it can cause irreversible impacts on ecosystems, calling the controversy over lithium 'dirty business for clean energy'. This means that advancing in the extraction requires large investments so that the risks of unwanted effects are mitigated, which seems crucial from the 'living well' perspective.

On the economic side, lithium is concentrated in a few regions. It is estimated that 70% of the total lithium available worldwide lies in South America, in the region of the Andean salt flats, referenced conventionally as the 'lithium triangle'. The market is quite restricted and access to these reserves is likely to bring about a new race for natural resources (Mining Dot Com 2018). Figure 5.3 shows the evolution of lithium carbonate prices for which in recent years the Chinese market has produced approximately 60% of the world's batteries.

With the beginning of the spread of EV, the price of lithium grew exponentially. However, at the end of 2018, prices dropped, leading some market analysts to suspect a lithium bubble (Sanderson 2017). Narins (2017) indicated that the lithium market is quite contradictory and that there is a tendency for the raw material price to drop related to the politicization around the exploration, the quality of the inputs, and the scarce existing infrastructure. Even so, lithium remains fundamental

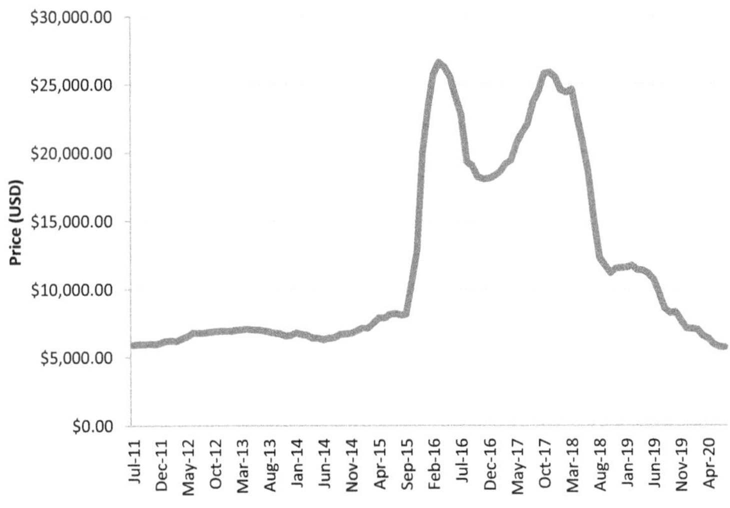

Figure 5.3 Lithium Carbonate 99.5%Min China Spot (price).
Source: authors elaboration from Investing (2020).

for battery production and geopolitical movements point to the expansion of its importance. According to the Global EV Outlook (IEA 2020), in international agreements to reduce CO_2 emissions, 17 countries have already announced their goal of transforming the vehicle fleet to 100% EV by 2050. To illustrate, a standard Tesla EV uses 63 kg of lithium carbonate, the equivalent to producing batteries for 10,000 smartphones (Engdahal 2019).

The development of greater capacity batteries proposes at least three other important impulses, mainly based on the possibilities generated by the dissemination of 5G technology. The first is the energy storage capacity in a decentralized way, which allows greater autonomy for local energy sovereignty and avoids the need to build large transmission infrastructure, in addition to encouraging generation through renewable means such as wind and photovoltaics (Goldthau 2014). The second is the military industry, which has increasingly relied on portable devices, such as drones, in a context called 'video game war' (Gregory 2011). The third is the axis of the production mode itself. In this case, given a system highly determined by the automation of productive processes, the organization of work tends to distance itself from formal hegemonic employment. The increase in the informality of the economy is the touchstone of this process, implying greater ungovernability over workers, a model that some authors call 'uberization' (Hughes and Southern 2019). In this scenario, the control capacity through portable devices that need to stay connected for extended periods and that requiring high capacity batteries will be increasingly linked to the process of governance and capital accumulation. Consequently, the race for lithium is closely linked to the reorganization of the global geopolitical space. Countries that have access to this natural resource may have a preponderance in the international division of labor in the new wave of microelectronic industrialization, often named the 'era of 5G' or the 'industry 4.0'.

The Bolivian lithium project

The exploitation of the metal in the lithium triangle region is more than 30 years old and the first prospects date back to the 1970s. However, given its characteristics in the Uyuni salt flat, attempts at the concession for exploration by transnational companies have not been successful (Bravo 2018). Many interpretations indicate that Bolivian lithium is very 'dirty', making the business inviable. Lithium is obtained through the evaporation of brines and the Bolivian brines are rich in four chemical components: Lithium, Magnesium, Potassium, and Boron. This makes the exploitation very expensive for market prospects. However, the increasing demand for lithium commodities is changing the prospects in favor of the viability of the Bolivian project.

The Uyuni Salt Flat is located in a highland that remained isolated with little road, electrical, and telecommunications infrastructure up until the Morales administration. Only with the arrival of MAS to power the lithium became an object of interest for the Development Plan. In 2008, the first more concrete steps were taken toward formulating a national plan of extraction. DS No. 29.496 declares the exploitation of evaporative resources as a national priority, creating the National Management for Evaporative Resources (GNRE) as a department of the Bolivian Mining Company (COMIBOL). The guidelines for the lithium exploration were determined in 2010 by GNRE, establishing the *National Strategy for the Industrialization of Evaporative Resources*, commanding the State to, in a sovereign way, research, explore, industrialize, and commercialize the resources. Ergo, all salt flats and salt lagoons have become national reserve areas, reversing previous concessions and prohibiting new ones (Bravo 2018).

In 2017, the lithium strategy left the Ministry of Mines and Metallurgy to be incorporated into the newly created Ministry of Energies (in plural). The National Strategic Public Company *Yacimientos de Litio Bolivianos* (YLB) was created, replacing GNRE. In short, the strategy is laid out on two grounds:

i All exploration of raw material, processing, and commercialization involving basic chemistry will be carried out only by the state company.
ii Processing residues, semi-industrialization, and industrialization can be carried out through association contracts with private national or foreign companies, provided that there is majority participation of the Bolivian State.

The strategy is based on four well-defined phases that pursue one clear objective: end-to-end industrialization, which constitutes the exception in relation to the way other countries in the region have launched themselves in this market (Ströbele-Gregor 2013; Revette, 2016; Fornillo 2018; Valenzuela 2020).

The *first phase* is configured as a process of research and development. Since 2008, the project has started to develop the technology to transform the brines into lithium carbonate, with viable methods. It begins with the experimentation of evaporation methods, goes through the construction of pilot plants and concludes with the establishment of two research centers for permanent technology development.

The *second phase* moves towards industrial-scale production. In 2013, the industrial brine pool structure for evaporation started to be built at the Uyuni Salt Flat – Llipi Plant – while complementing the industrialization of brine through the construction of Potassium Chloride (KCl) and Lithium Carbonate (Li_2CO_3) Industrial Plants. The *third phase* is designed to add value to the lithium industry by industrializing the production residues from the Llipi Plant to produce lithium-ion batteries and cathodic materials. This phase is carried out at La Palca, 200 km from the Uyuni Salt Flat, in association with private companies with the necessary technological capacity. The *fourth phase* is intended to industrialize other Bolivian salt flats, mainly the Coipasa and Pastos Grandes. In this phase, the association with private companies is also foreseen so that there is greater added value in production. Figure 5.4 shows the salt flats and plants of lithium's strategy.

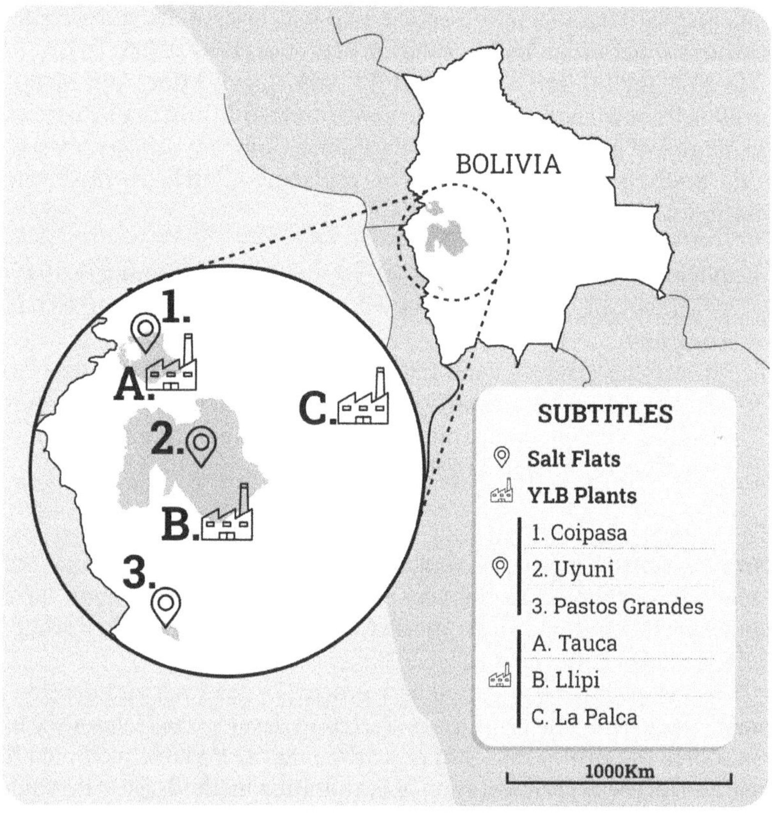

Figure 5.4 Bolivian Lithium's Map.
Source: authors elaboration.

Progress and challenges

Morales believed that by seizing the 'comparative advantage' of having the largest reserves of lithium in the world, it would be possible to promote industrialization through external partners and transform Bolivia into a big player in this market. The lithium industrialization strategy was guided by a kind of market reserve that, for ten years, built the conditions to achieve bargaining power in the international market.

The *first phase* project was concluded with relative success, achieving a structure for research and development of the chemical industry that is unique in Latin America (Bravo 2018), and developing the necessary technology to extract lithium from specific brines in Bolivian salt flats. In this context, agreements were also signed with Bolivian universities for innovation and patent registration. The *second phase* is partially completed. The industrial pools are already working with more than 60% of the capacity, with just a few pending phases. The KCl industrial plant was opened in 2018, having a production capacity of 350,000 tons per year. The Li_2CO_3 Industrial Plant is in the final stage of construction, scheduled for completion in 2020. Once in operation, it will be able to produce 15,000 tons per year.

YLB expected that by 2025 Bolivia would be able to produce 200 thousand tons of lithium commodities. A market of almost 2 billion dollars,[8] equivalent to approximately 5% of the current Bolivian GDP, this level of production would position Bolivia as a player in the international lithium market. China, the largest lithium consumer in the world, estimates that it will demand 800 thousand tons of lithium in 2025, which presents a promising scenario for Bolivia if the state company YLB manages to complete the third and fourth phases by that time. To advance the *third phase*, Bolivia needs to negotiate agreements with foreign companies on the basis of the strategy:

a The Bolivian State will be the majority shareholder;
b The company must demonstrate a high technological capacity;
c The company must guarantee the market for all production;
d The raw material available is only the residual brine from the production processes carried out by YLB.

Partly stimulated by the high prices due to the Chinese demand, Bolivia formed a mixed company between YLB (51%) and the German company ACI System (49%) in 2018, for a duration of 70 years, with the ambition to export Bolivian batteries to the European market by 2023. The aim is to construct three industrial plants for the production of Lithium Hydroxide (LiOH), from residual brines; cathodic materials; and batteries.

First steps have also been taken to advance to the *fourth phase*. On August 20, 2019, a preliminary agreement of a mixed company was signed between YLB and the Chinese Xinjiang TBEA Group, to industrialize the Coipasa and Pastos Grandes' salt flats: partnership still under negotiation that foresees the construction of seven industrial plants, with an investment of around US$ 2,3 billion.

The lithium industrialization strategy breaks with the traditional logic of the export of raw materials as it aims to create an endogenization process of the battery production chain in a sovereign way. Although the expected growing demand for lithium supports this plan, the development of the industry still faces many uncertainties. The battery market tends to accelerate its demands as EVs spread, and Bolivia still needs to take some important steps to successfully position itself in the international arena. Entering the hegemonic dispute in one of the most dynamic markets in the world without a competitive technological foundation is a very high bet. The absence of a sovereign exit to the sea is another aggravating factor in this process. It means that being part of the global value chain that is at the heart of the contemporary global energy transition requires very efficient logistics. At the moment, Bolivia is isolated, without direct access to markets. A third pungent issue relates to the absence of qualified labor to take on the highly specialized jobs that the sector requires. Brugger and Zamora (2014) indicate how this issue can impact the possibilities for advancing the lithium project. In Uyuni, it was only in 2019 that the first Technology Institute for the training of qualified workers was opened. The education to qualified labor is a lengthy process and in a fast-developing market, Bolivia may not get there in time.

Despite the recognition of these difficulties, an agreement was reached with the German company to advance the project. In the dispute between the United States and China, which controls most of the lithium market, Germany, which aims to advance its EVs fleet, found itself without access to raw materials for the production of batteries. Making the agreement with Bolivia was a way to remain in the dispute, even accepting the high Bolivian conditions.

Lithium, geopolitics, and coup d'etat

In an interview with Russian media Sputnik News (2019), two months after the turbulent Bolivian elections of October 20, 2019, US Republican Senator Richard Black declared

> I think there was concern on our part that the Chinese might begin to exert influence within Bolivia. And that it might have somehow made it more difficult for the United States to obtain lithium

> for batteries that we're now using in automobiles… I think it was part of the equation at least.

This was said amid discussions about the intervening role in Latin America that his country's government seems to have resumed under President Trump's 'America First' doctrine.

The hegemonic narrative about the 2019 elections does not deal with the issue of possible US intervention. For the dominant communication channels, Morales' resignation was the result of legitimate internal movements of the Bolivian middle class against Morales' perpetuation in power and alleged fraud in the election. This was only put in check in June 2020, when the New York Times released a scientific report (Idrobo et al. 2020) that indicated the inconsistency of the fraud assumption in the OAS audit over the elections (Kurmanaev and Trigo 2020).

For our interpretation, that understands this process as a coup d'etat, it is essential to comprehend Bolivia's attempt at insertion in a global market on the basis of sovereignty and explicit anti-imperialist rhetoric. The case of lithium is emblematic in this regard. Morales' power was directly linked to the idea of governing by social movements, which conjectures an extraordinary force to establish a sovereign project. Beyond this, the strategy of macroeconomic pragmatism prevented most foreign interventions through the financial market, effectively defying the imperialist technological monopoly. Every system is controlled by rules that guarantee the maintenance of the transnational companies' hegemony through patents. According to Veltmeyer and Petras (2019) there is permanent control over innovation in a monopoly of brainpower, and the unfeasibility of new technologies that threaten such hegemony. The authors call this the Imperial Innovation System.

It took Bolivia almost ten years to organize the necessary conditions for the primary processing of brines and managed to develop the initial evaporation and processing methods. It also managed to build a national integration infrastructure capable of making the project viable. With that, it was hoped to reach more advantageous agreements for the other industrialization stages, in which there could be technology transfer, to avoid the transnationals' access to raw material without added value.

Although Bolivia managed to circumvent to a certain extent the technological, financial, and natural resources monopolies, a break with communications and military monopolies has not been achieved. Despite attempts to reduce the influence of the dominant media and to build sovereignty within the armed forces through the establishment of an anti-imperialist military school; the practical results of these measures have been minimal. The political crisis that was initiated at the end of 2019 needs also to be understood in the context of a hegemonic dispute between the United States and China, i.e. the Chinese expansion since the beginning of the century and the consequent reaction by the United States to resume its influence in the region. The Chinese expansion in Latin America is centered on expanding credit availability through Chinese development banks and Foreign Direct Investment (FDI), mainly in the construction of infrastructure, as part of the Belt and Road Initiative (BRI). For Baiyi (2016), Chinese cooperation is established to raise the Chinese companies' position in global value chains and ensure the external supply of raw materials and commodities.

For Bolivia, China seems to occupy the space of main strategic partner, as illustrated by the signing of several bilateral agreements. This is evident in a series of strategic partnership agreements signed between countries on a bilateral basis. An amount of US$ 1.7 billion was sent for development assistance and the execution of 11 major infrastructure works (Koleski and Blivas 2018), indicating the Chinese interest in gaining access to Bolivia's natural resources. Lithium seems to be central. In addition to the principle of the agreement established with YLB for the *fourth phase* of the Bolivian lithium strategy, the construction of the industrial plants in the Uyuni Salt Flat was carried out by Chinese companies (YLB 2020).

The Chinese 'invasion' in Latin America is the touchstone of the reaction that the United States has established for the region. The US interference in Bolivia is historic, mainly around the alleged confrontation with narco organizations (drug traffic) that masked the interests in accessing natural resources. Quintana (2016) indicates this process, exposing its most recent context in 'Bolivialeaks'. Besides, since 2013, the impetus to destabilization movements in Latin America has been fostered by US-based institutions, such as Atlas Network (Macedo 2018). In this sense, Trump's rise is symbolic, presenting a more explicit version of a 'New Monroe Doctrine'. After the Pink Tide, Latin America has moved towards the right, under US aligned presidencies such as those of Jair Bolsonaro and Sebastián Piñera. For Veltmeyer and Petras (2019: 130), this resumption allowed Trump to preside over all of America, with a few exceptions. The intervention system, in a kind of conservative restoration – with hints of fascism in direct clash with progressive agendas – is justified by the supposed need to retake democracy in the region against the Chinese imperialist rise. As a result, electoral systems in many countries have been occupied by Trump's allies, with political victories that have generally been marked by illicit means, controversial elections, fraught with violence, corruption, and US complicity (ibid.).

At the end of 2019, Bolivia was violently inserted into this process. The destabilization experienced since 2019 substantiates the discussion around imperialism and the hegemonic dispute. The Lithium project was one of the determining fronts of the coup, where business movements in the Potosi region demanded better royalties for the Department, the cancelation of the association with the German company and Morales' resignation. The plan for battery production was suspended as a result.

However, the 'New Monroe Doctrine' seems to be in crisis as a new progressive wave (re)awakes in Latin America. Next to left wing governments in Mexico and Argentina, Ecuador and Colombia are facing constant popular movements and social protest against neoliberalism. Venezuela, despite the very serious political, economic, and social crisis, continues to resist US imperialism. In Chile, popular pressure has just called a popular constituent through a plebiscite, and in Bolivia, MAS has seen a historic political turnaround in which the coup was defeated massively at the ballot box.

The industrialization of lithium remains the bet for an emancipated future for Bolivia. Luis Arce won the elections promising to continue the 'process of change' and economic recovery. The president indicated his anti-imperialist stance and was averse to access any support coming from international institutions determined by the logic of North American imperialism, such as the IMF, which, during the coup process, carried out financing operations for the Áñez government.

On the other hand, partnerships with China set the tone for the Bolivian recovery. Notwithstanding the contradictions that arise from the combination of a socialist and capitalist model, within the framework of harmonic development that supposedly guides its expansion model, at least for the time being, China has demonstrated to be a different kind of world power. The Chinese expansion model does not align with imperialism as it was established in the history of capitalism (Lopes Ribeiro 2017). Thus, for the continuation of lithium industrialization, Bolivia seems to be open to restarting the partnership with the Germans, who are eager to resume their access to the natural resource. The Bolivian government's need to balance tensions in the Potosí region may lead to higher conditions around the lithium royalties, but if the Germans do not accept the new requirements, the Chinese may be willing to step in. In the global pandemic scenario, China is the country that presents a more accelerated recovery and Beijing's ambitions regarding EV are wide (Kuo 2020; Kynge 2020).

Conclusion

The overwhelming victory in the October 2020 elections demonstrated that the majority of Bolivians voted for the continuation of the MAS political project of building a sovereign country. The strategy of nominating as a candidate a politician considered moderate, despite being committed to the historic struggles of the Bolivian popular movements, managed to gather the absolute majority of voters in the idea of recovering the positive balance of the Morales administration. This, in addition to the political, economic, and health disaster of the coup administration, led the economist Luis Arce to the government, with the mission of renewing and advancing the project that started in 2006. A proposal for continuity and change at the same time.

In the election campaign, Arce indicated that the lithium industrialization project would be resumed as a priority in his government and from there the great reconstruction of the country would be established. However, due to specific current circumstances – the coup, economic destruction, and the health crisis – the lithium project may be pressured to respond quickly to the ailments of the crises. As lithium exploration has not yet completed its planned structure, tensions will likely be exacerbated towards an austere solution. It will be up to the struggle of organized workers and the people to resist, in the face of imperialist intentions, to uphold the transition to their emancipation. Because the government alone, as history has shown, is not able to withstand the global capital vortex.

Notes

1 Cf. <https://twitter.com/elonmusk/status/1287578839821033472>. Musk deleted the publication and in the next day published, as a provocation, a song by the North American group Nirvana called 'Lithium'. Perhaps the CEO is really interested in lithium carbonate, but not to produce batteries for electric cars, who knows the goal is to treat bipolar disorder, as told by the story of the composition of this song by Kurt Cobain.

2 US$ 3,548.59 in 2019 (World Bank 2020).

3 It is interesting to note that, despite the proximity to the neo-structuralist ideas that somehow permanently dialogued with the country projects of the governments of the progressive wave in Latin America, in Bolivia, there is a more intense tendency in the dialogue with authors of the so-called world-system theory, whose origin in the region occurs in the Marxist theory of dependence. A symbol of this perspective is that the Central Bank of Bolivia Seminars is named Theotônio dos Santos, one of the most important authors of the Marxist theory of dependence.

4 These processes were often marked by conflicts. The contract renewal with the Brazilian oil company 'Petrobrás' for gas exploration in the Bolivian East, for example, was immersed in important political and

economic disputes, but which in the end enabled a greater benefit for the country (Fuser 2015).

5 At the beginning of the 21st century, Brazil discovered an enormous amount of hydrocarbons present in underground lands at the bottom of the Atlantic Ocean off the Brazilian coast and developed technology for their extraction (PETROBRAS n.d.).

6 For gas industrialization, only the urea and ammoniac factory in Bulo Bulo – Cochabamba comprised an investment of almost US$ 1,000 million. Having been inaugurated 2017, with a diary production capacity of 2,100 tons of fertilizers (Castro et al. 2020).

7 The problem is that today the global energy mix is still based mainly on fossil fuels.

8 The price of lithium is around US$ 9,500 per ton on the world market, according to data from S&P Global.

References

Albó, X. (2008) *Movimientos y poder indígena en Bolivia*. CIPCA, La Paz.

Amin, S. (1989) *El eurocentrismo*: critica de una ideología. Siglo XXI, Mexico DF.

———. (2003) *Obsolescent Capitalism*. Zed books, London.

———. (2014) 'Contra Hardt and Negri: multitude or generalized proletarization', *Monthly Review* 66, no. 6 (November), https://monthlyreview.org/2014/11/01/contra-hardt-and-negri/

———. (2015) 'Contemporary imperialism', *Montly Review* 67, no. 3 (July–August), https://monthlyreview.org/2015/07/01/contemporary-imperialism/

Arce Catacora, L. A. (2011) 'El Nuevo Modelo Económico, Social, Comunitario y Productivo', *Economia Plural* 1 (September): 3–12, https://repositorio.economiayfinanzas.gob.bo/documentos/2018/UCS/materiales Elaborados/publicaciones/Revista_01.pdf

Baiyi, W. et al. (2016) *Oportunidades em meio á transformação*: uma análise multidimensional das perspectivas de cooperação entre China e América Latina. Cultura Acadêmica, São Paulo.

Bolivia (2006) Decreto Supremo no. 28701, https://www.ypfb.gob.bo/es/component/phocadownload/category/7-leyes-y-decretos-de-nacionalizacion.html?download=15:ds-29189

——— (2008) Decreto Supremo no. 29496, http://www.mineria.gob.bo/juridica/20080401-9-53-43.pdf

——— (2009) Constitución Política del Estado, https://sea.gob.bo/digesto/CompendioNormativo/01.pdf

Bravo, J. C. M. (2018) 'El modelo de industrialización del litio en Bolivia', *Revista de ciencias sociales* 10, no. 34 (September): 69–82, http://ridaa.unq.edu.ar/handle/20.500.11807/1736

Brugger, F. and Zamora, K. L (2014) 'Why commodity booms have not (yet?) Boosted human capital: Bolivia's struggle to create a skilled workforce', in G. Carbonnier, M. Carton and K. King (eds) *Education, Learning, Training: Critical Issues for Development*, pp81–101. Brill, Leiden | Boston.

Castro, F. S. M., Guerra, S. M. G. and Lima Filho, P. A. (2020) 'Bolívia pré-golpe: notas de um estudo de campo', *Revista Fim do Mundo* 1 (January–April): 104–133, https://doi.org/10.36311/2675-3871.2020.v1n01.p104-133

Castro, N. and Rosental, R. (2017) 'The Bolivian electricity sector and perspectives for integration with Brazil', *GESEL*, http://www.gesel.ie.ufrj.br/app/webroot/files/IFES/BV/castro170_ing.pdf

ENDE (2018) Memoria anual ENDE 2018, https://www.ende.bo/public/memorias/memoria2018.pdf

Engdahal, F. W. (2019) 'China, USA and the geopolitics of lithium', *New Eastern Outlook*, https://journal-neo.org/2019/11/18/china-usa-and-the-geopolitics-of-lithium/

Farah H., I. and Vasapollo, L. (2016) 'Introducción', in I. Farah H., and L. Vasapollo (eds) *Vivir Bien: ¿Paradigma no capitalista?*, pp11–35. CIDES-UMSA, La Paz.

Fernandes, F. (1976) *A revolução burguesa no Brasil*. 2nd ed. Zahar Editores, Rio de Janeiro.

Fornillo, B. (2018). 'La energía del litio en Argentina y Bolivia: comunidad, extractivismo y posdesarrollo', *Colombia Internacional* 93 (January–March): 179–201, https://dx.doi.org/10.7440/colombiaint93.2018.07

Fuser, I. (2015) *As Razões da Bolívia*: dinheiro e poder no conflito com a Petrobras pelo controle do gás natural (2003–2007). Editora UFABC, Santo André.

Goldthau, A. (2014) 'Rethinking the governance of energy infrastructure: scale, decentralization and polycentrism', *Energy Research and Social Science* 1: 134–140, https://doi.org/10.1016/j.erss.2014.02.009

Gouze, A. (2010) 'Le lithium: un métal stratégique', *Responsabilité & Environnement* 58 (April): 84–91, http://www.annales.org/re/2010/re58/Gouze.pdf

Gregory, D. (2011) 'From a view to a kill: Drones and late modern war', *Culture & Society* 28 (July – August): 188–215, https://doi.org/10.1177/0263276411423027

Gudynas, E. (2011) 'Tensiones, contradicciones y oportunidades de la dimensión ambiental del Buen Vivir', in I. Farah H., and L. Vasapollo (eds) *Vivir Bien*: ¿Paradigma no capitalista?, pp231–246. CIDES-UMSA, La Paz.

Harvey, D. (2003) *The New Imperialism*. Oxford University Press, Oxford.

Hughes, C. and Southern, A. (2019) 'The world of work and the crisis of capitalism: Marx and the Fourth Industrial Revolution', *Educational Researcher* 19, no. 1: 508–514, doi: 10.3102/0013189X16683408

Idrobo, N., Kronick, D. and Rodríguez, F. (2020) 'Do shifts in late-counted votes signal fraud? Evidence from Bolivia', University of Pennsylvania. SSRN (June): 1–47, https://ssrn.com/abstract=3621475

IEA (2020) 'Global EV outlook 2020. Entering the decade of electric drive?', Technology report, https://www.iea.org/reports/global-ev-outlook-2020

IMF (2018) 'IMF Executive Board Concludes 2018. Article IV. Consultation with Bolivia', https://www.imf.org/en/News/Articles/2018/12/06/pr18453-imf-executive-board-concludes-2018-article-iv-consultation-with-bolivia

INE (2020) 'Estadisticas econômicas', https://www.ine.gob.bo/index.php/estadisticas-economicas/

Investing (2020) Lithium carbonate 99.5% min China spot, https://www.investing.com/commodities/lithium-carbonate-99.5-min-china-futures, accessed July 10, 2020

Katz, C. (2015) 'La sorpresa de Bolivia', *Nómadas, Critical Journal of Social and Juridical Sciences* 44, no. 4: 5–16, https://doi.org/10.5209/rev_NOMA.2014.v44.n4.49289

Koleski, K. and Blivas, A. (2018) 'China's Engagement with Latin America and the Caribbean', U.S. – China Economic and Security Review Commission. Staff Research Report, https://www.uscc.gov/research/chinas-engagement-latin-america-and-caribbean

Kuo, L. (2020) 'China becomes first major economy to recover from Covid-19 pandemic', *The Guardian*, 19 October, https://www.theguardian.com/business/2020/oct/19/china-becomes-first-major-economy-to-recover-from-covid-19-pandemic

Kurmanaev, A. and Trigo, M. S. (2020) 'A bitter election. Accusations of fraud. And now second thoughts', *The New York Times*, 7 June, https://www.nytimes.com/2020/06/07/world/americas/bolivia-election-evo-morales.html

Kynge, J. (2020) 'China races ahead in electric vehicles', *Financial Times*, 28 October, https://www.ft.com/content/f414839d-b7e0-43ea-bba2-dc8966d64a11

Lalander, R. (2016) 'Ethnic rights and the dilemma of extractive development in plurinational Bolivia', *The International Journal of Human Rights* 21, no. 4 (May): 464–481, https://doi.org/10.1080/13642987.2016.1179869

Lambert, R. (2019) 'En Bolivie, un coup d'État trop facile', Le Monde Diplomatic, 9 December, https://www.monde-diplomatique.fr/2019/12/LAMBERT/61150

Linera, A. G. (2018) *O que é uma Revolução*? Expressão Popular, São Paulo.

——— (2019) *Tensões Criativas da Revolução*. Expressão Popular, São Paulo.

Lopes Ribeiro, V. (2017) 'A expansão chinesa recente e novas determinações do imperialismo no século XXI', *Estudos Internacionais*: Revista de Relações Internacionais da PUC Minas 5, no. 1: 121–140, https://doi.org/10.5752/P.2317-773X.2017v5n1p121

Löwy, M (2003) *O Pensamento de Che Guevara*. Expressão Popular, São Paulo.

Macedo, E. (2018) 'Repoliticizing the social and taking liberty back', *Educação em Revista* 34 (October): 1–15, https://doi.org/10.1590/0102-4698212010

Mining Dot Com (2018) 'The international lithium race', Resources Monitor, April 4, https://www.mining.com/web/international-lithium-race/

MMAyA (2017) Plan Sectorial de Desarrollo Integral del Ministerio de Medio Ambiente y Agua, https://www.mmaya.gob.bo/wp-content/uploads/2019/06/PLAN_SECTORIAL_DE_DESARROLLO_INTEGRAL_DEL_MMAyA-PSDI_20-04-2017-1.pdf

Morales Ayma, E. (2011) 'Prólogo'. in I. Farah H., and L. Vasapollo (eds) *Vivir Bien*: ¿Paradigma no capitalista?, pp7–10. CIDES-UMSA, La Paz.

Narins, T. P (2017). 'The battery business: Lithium availability and the growth of the global electric car industry', *The Extractive Industries and Society* 4, no. 2 (April): 321–328, https://doi.org/10.1016/j.exis.2017.01.013

Nascimento, A. (2016) *O genocídio do negro brasileiro*: processo de um racismo mascarado. Editora Perspectiva, São Paulo.

PETOBRAS (n.d.) 'Pre-Salt', https://petrobras.com.br/en/our-activities/performance-areas/oil-and-gas-exploration-and-production/pre-salt/

Postero, N. (2017) *The Indigenous State: Race, Politics, and Performance in Plurinational Bolivia*. University of California Press, Oakland/California.

Quintana Taborga, J.R. (ed) (2016) *BoliviaLeaks: La injerencia política de Estados Unidos contra el proceso de cambio (2006–2010)*. PIEB, La Paz.

Ranta, E. (2016) 'Vivir bien governance in Bolivia: chimera or attainable utopia?', *Third World Quarterly* 38, no. 7 (October): 1603–1618, https://doi.org/10.1080/01436597.2016.1224551

Revette, A. C. (2016) 'This time it's different: Lithium extraction, cultural politics and development in Bolivia', *Third World Quarterly* 38, no. 1 (February): 149–168, https://doi.org/10.1080/01436597.2015.1131118

Roca Sánchez, M. A. (2017) *Proceso de cambio: el milagro que no fue*. Fundación Vicente Pazoskanki, La Paz.

Sanderson, H. (2017) 'Lithium: The next speculative bubble?', *Financial Times*, 6 January, https://www.ft.com/content/4fd165d6-d274-11e6-9341-7393bb2e1b51

Sputnik News (2019) 'US must let Venezuelans, Bolivians sort out their own governments – Senator', opinion, 10 December, https://sputniknews.com/analysis/201912101077528212-us-must-let-venezuelans-bolivians-sort-out-their-own-governments-state-senator/

Stefanoni, P. (2012) '¿Y quién no querría "vivir bien"? Encrucijadas del proceso de cambio boliviano', *Crítica y Emancipación* 4, no. 7 (January–July): 9–25, http://bibliotecavirtual.clacso.org.ar/clacso/se/20120605025226/CyE7.pdf

Ströbele-Gregor, J. (2013) 'El proyecto estatal del litio en Bolivia: Expectativas, desafíos y dilemas', *Nueva Sociedad* 244 (March–April): 74–83, https://www.nuso.org/media/articles/downloads/3929_1.pdf

Takemura, N. (2018) 'Lithium Extraction at the Salar de Uyuni in Bolivia: 'Dirty business for clean energy' emancipates Bolivia from 'curse'?' *Research Bulletin* 38 (June): 31–38, https://toin.repo.nii.ac.jp/?action=repository_uri&item_id=278&file_id=22&file_no=1

Valenzuela, J. R. (2020) *Natural Resource Governance, Grievances and Conflict: The Case of the Bolivian Lithium Program*. Springer VS, Berlin.

Veltmeyer, H. and Petras, J. (2019) *Latin America in the Vortex of Social Change*. Routledge, London | New York.

World Bank (2020) World Bank open data, https://data.worldbank.org/

YLB (2020) 'Audiencia Pública de Rendición de cuentas Final 2019 e Inicial 2020', ylb.gob.bo/resources/rendicion_cuentas/rendicion_inicial_2020.pdf

Zavaleta Mercado, R. (1990) *La formación de la conciencia nacional*. Los amigos del libro, Cochabamba.

Index

Note: **Bold** page numbers refer to tables, *italic* page numbers refer to figures and page numbers followed by "n" refer to end notes.

For Product Safety Concerns and Information please contact our EU representative GPSR@taylorandfrancis.com
Taylor & Francis Verlag GmbH, Kaufingerstraße 24, 80331 München, Germany

www.ingramcontent.com/pod-product-compliance
Ingram Content Group UK Ltd.
Pitfield, Milton Keynes, MK11 3LW, UK
UKHW021956180926
475701UK00003B/59
9780367707743